Workbook to Accompany

The Legal Research and Writing Handbook

A Basic Approach for Paralegals

Second Edition

Andrea B. Yelin

Hope Viner Samborn

Aspen Law & Business
A Division of Aspen Publishers, Inc.
Gaithersburg   New York

ISBN 0 - 7355 - 0297 - 8

Permissions
Aspen Law & Business
A Division of Aspen Publishers, Inc.
1185 Avenue of the Americas
New York, NY 10036

1 2 3 4 5

Contents

Introduction

This workbook contains exercises to hone your research and writing skills. Neither subject can be learned without continuous experience in these areas. To learn how to research a topic effectively, you must work with library resources and develop an understanding of how they can best serve your needs. Writing skills also must be developed with practice.

The text, *The Legal Research and Writing Handbook, 2nd Edition,* provides the foundation. After you have read the text, you should understand how the library resources can assist you in your research projects and how to use each of the sources presented. However, your understanding of these materials will be heightened if you use these sources yourself to experience how each resource looks, its organization and relationship to the other materials. The text also will provide you with a framework for legal writing projects. You must reinforce these concepts by performing the additional exercises provided in the workbook.

The workbook exercises are divided into two sections. For most chapters, the first set of exercises is labeled basic concepts that test your understanding of the topic definitions in each chapter. You should test your knowledge of each concept by completing these exercises before working on the second set of exercises. If you find that you do not understand a concept, re-read the appropriate text section before completing the second set of exercises.

The second group of questions called application of concepts will allow you to use the information gleaned from each chapter to solve a research or writing problem. These exercises are similar in design to assignments you might receive as practicing paralegals. The research exercises will enable you to organize your research and writing projects. They also will allow you to become familiar with each library resource and to understand how to use library resources can be used in conjunction with each other. When you finish these exercises, you should have reinforced your understanding of the concepts presented in the text and be able to complete research assignments as a practicing paralegal. The writing exercises also will bolster your understanding of the writing concepts you will have learned from the text.

The exercises are structured to assist you in understanding the research and writing process. Note the questions because they often are basic questions you should ask yourself when you begin or work through any research or writing project. Although many projects require you to work in a law library, we have included some exercises that use the illustrations contained in the text for those of you who may have limited law library access.

Good luck with these projects. We hope you enjoy doing the exercises and learn to hone your research and writing skills. We also hope that these projects will help you when you begin to practice as paralegals.

Andrea B. Yelin
Hope Viner Samborn

Chapter 1
The Legal System

Basic Concepts Exercises

Government Questions:

1.   What are the branches of the U.S. government and what are the responsibilities of each branch?

2.   Can the Arizona Legislature adopt a law that contradicts the U.S. Constitution?

3.   What are Congress-created laws called?

4.   Briefly how does Congress create a law?

5.   What government agencies handle day-to-day regulatory issues?

6.   How are administrative agencies empowered?

7.   What are the trial courts of the United States called?

8.   What U.S. court is the highest court?

9.   What is the body of law created by the courts called?

10.   Do appellate courts generally decide issues of fact?

11.   How is the legal system organized in the United States?

12.   What bodies comprise the U.S. government, and what body of law defines their relationship to each other?

13.   What government bodies are part of the legislative branch, and what do they do?

14.   What comprises the executive branch?

15.   What is the federal court system, and what are its duties?

16.   What do the trial courts do?

17.   What is the U.S. Supreme Court, and what does it do?

18.   Can state courts decide issues of federal law?

19.   Can federal courts decide issues of state law?

Application of Basic Research Concepts Exercises

1.   Draw a diagram of your state court system.

2.   Diagram how a case would go through the system you diagrammed in Question 1.

3.   Draw a flow chart of how a case would go through the federal court system.

Chapter 2
What Law Governs

Basic Concept Exercises

Governing Law Questions

1.   Can state courts decide issues of federal law?

2.   Can federal courts decide issues of state law?

3.   Must the U.S. Circuit of Appeals for the Ninth Circuit follow a decision of the U.S. Supreme Court concerning a federal issue?

4.   Must an Arkansas trial court follow a decision of the U.S. Supreme Court concerning an issue of federal law?

5.   What is precedent and why is it important?

6.   What is dicta and when is it important?

7.   What are your research goals?

8.   What is primary authority?

9.   What is binding or mandatory authority?

10.   When would you use primary authority?

11. What is secondary authority?

12. When would you use secondary authority?

13. If you have found both a primary binding authority and a secondary authority which apply to your legal question, which would you use and why?

14. If you have a primary binding authority and a primary persuasive authority, which authority would you use and why?

15. If you have a primary persuasive authority and a secondary authority, which would you use and why?

16. If you have a primary binding authority and dicta, which would you use and why?

17. If you have a primary persuasive authority and dicta, which would you use and why?

18. If you have a secondary authority and dicta, which would you use and why?

19. Are all secondary authorities given the same weight by the courts?

20. Will you always find a primary or secondary authority which is relevant to your case?

21. How do you use dicta?

22. How do you determine what law governs your case?

23. What is jurisdiction?

24. What factors determine what jurisdiction governs your case, and should you make that determination?

25. After you have determined the jurisdiction, how do you determine what cases or laws control the outcome of your research issue?

26. What is the hierarchy of legal authorities?

27. Do decisions of the federal trial courts, appellate courts and the U.S. Supreme Court carry the same weight?

28. Within the federal system, how does this hierarchy operate?

29. Can decisions of courts concerning the same issue differ between circuits?

30. If two appellate courts have conflicting decisions concerning the same issue, how can you as researchers decide what law governs?

31. How does the hierarchy of authority work when you have both state and federal decisions concerning an issue?

32. Does the authority of the federal and state governments ever conflict?

33. When the highest court of one state decides an issue, must the state court in another state follow that decision?

34. How do you understand a court decision and its impact on a case?

35. Why is precedent important?

36. Does every statement made in a court decision have the force of law?

37.   If dicta is not binding, why is it important?

38.   How do you determine whether a case is mandatory or binding authority?

39.   Is all primary authority mandatory or binding?

40.   When is an authority merely persuasive?

Application of Basic Research Concepts Exercises

1.   You are a paralegal in the state in which you live. You have been assigned to research whether an individual can bring an action in state court against a car dealer and the car manufacturer of a car which has been trouble-ridden since the individual purchased it eight months ago.

Part A   Research Strategy and Goals

a.   Does federal or state law govern this question?

b.   If state law governs, what is the jurisdiction and why?

c.   What type of authority would you be seeking and why?

d.   Who creates the authorities you would be seeking?

Part B   Understanding Your Research Results

You have completed your research. You have found a statute which explains lemon law actions in your state, two cases in your state which interpret the statute, a federal case which explains the lemon law's application in your state, a case from another state which explains the lemon law, an encyclopedia explanation of the statute, a periodical article in a bar journal about lemon law actions in your state and a newspaper article which explains how to bring a lemon law action and what actions are barred.

a.   What type of authority is the lemon law statute in your state?

b.   What type of authority are the two cases from your state?

c.   What type of authority is the case from another state?

d.   What type of authority is the federal case?

e.   What type of authority is the encyclopedia reference to the statute?

f.   What type of authority is the periodical article?

g.   What type of authority is the newspaper article?

h.   Which, if any, authorities might be binding or mandatory authorities?

i.   Which authorities might be noted in a memorandum to a court?

j.   Rank the authorities according to whether they are primary mandatory, primary persuasive or secondary authorities and which authorities you would use first, second, third and so on, if at all. (Some authorities could be in multiple positions. Use your best judgment to select only one spot for each authority.) If you would not use an authority, list why not. Explain why you rank an authority in a particular position.

2.   You are a paralegal who has been asked to research whether a state government violated the federal Americans with Disabilities Act when it failed to redesign its courtroom to accommodate wheel chairs.

Part A   Research Strategy and Goals

a.   Does federal or state law govern?

b.   What is the jurisdiction and why?

c.   What type of authority would you be seeking and why?

d.   Who creates the authorities you would be seeking?

Part B   Understanding Your Research Results

You have completed your research. You have found a federal statute that concerns redesigning buildings to accommodate disable persons. You have found a U.S. Supreme Court case which addresses the question of state government agencies redesigning existing buildings. The decision was made on February 25, 1998. You also have found the statute that was adopted before the Supreme Court case on January 15, 1998. You have found an article in the National Law Journal, a legal trade newspaper, which explains the redesign issue as it relates to state governments and a federal administrative regulation concerning redesigning courtrooms. In addition, you have a state court decision in which the state supreme court in your state decided that state governments do not have to comply with the federal statute.

a.   What type of authority is the statute?

b.   What type of authority is the state court case from your state?

c.   What type of authority is the U.S. Supreme Court case?

d.   What type of authority is the National Law Journal article?

e.   What type of authority is the federal administrative regulation?

f.   Rank the authorities and list whether the authority is a primary binding or persuasive authority or whether it is a secondary authority. Explain why you rank the authority in its position.

3.   You are a paralegal in Texas who has been asked to research whether a physician specialist in cardiology is held to a local or national standard of care in treating a cardiac patient.

You are preparing a research memorandum that will be used as a basis for defending an action against a Texas doctor in a Texas state court.

Part A   *Research Strategy and Goals*

a.   What is the jurisdiction and why?

b.   What type of authority would you be seeking and why?

c.   Who creates the authorities you would be seeking?

Part B   *Understanding Your Research Results*

Briefly explain when or why you would use each source listed below. Indicate whether it is a primary or secondary authority and whether it is binding or persuasive.

a.   An American Jurisprudence 2d encyclopedia section on physician malpractice generally.

b.   A Texas Supreme Court case on point.

c.   An Illinois state Supreme Court case on point

d.   A U.S. Supreme Court Case

e.   A U.S. District Court case for the Northern District of Ohio

f.   A U.S. District Court Case for the Northern District of Illinois

4.   Which of the following decisions would be binding precedent upon the United States Court of Appeals for the Seventh Circuit located in Chicago regarding an issue of federal law?

a.   A decision of the United States Supreme Court.
b.   A decision of a United States Court of Appeals for the Fifth Circuit.
c.   A decision of the United States District Court located in Chicago.
d.   a and b only.
e.   all of the above

5.   Which of the following decisions would be binding upon the United States Court of Appeals for the Tenth Circuit regarding an issue of federal law?

a.   A decision of the United States Supreme Court
b.   A decision of the United States Seventh Circuit Court of Appeals located in Chicago
c.   A decision of the Colorado Supreme Court
d.   all of the above
e.   a and b only

Basic Concepts Exercises

1.   What is case law?

2.   What government body generates case law?

3.   What is the national reporter system?

4.   How are case reporters organized?

5.   What is a slip opinion?

6.   Where would you find a U.S. Supreme Court slip opinion?

7.   List three sources for other slip opinions.

8.   What are advance sheets?

9.   What is a reporter?

10.   List three reporters which contain U.S. Supreme Court opinions.

11.   What is a regional reporter?

12.   What is the difference between an official reporter and an unofficial reporter?

13.   Do all states have official reporters?

14.   What is a headnote?

15.   What is the value of a headnote?

16.   What is a key number?

17.   How and why would you use a key number?

18.   Can you find federal and state court decisions on the Internet?

19.   Do any publishers besides West Group use headnotes?

20.   Other than online on the major legal research services or in hardcopy case reporters, where would you find court decisions?

21.   Where would you find unpublished case decisions? List at least two sources.

22.   List three methods for using the digests.

23.   Who writes the headnotes and when, if at all, would you cite one?

24.   Where in a digest would you find the most current cases?

Application of Digest Concepts Exercises

1.   Review Illustration 3-7 in the text. Under what topic and key number in the Ohio digest would you find cases that are likely to illustrate the point of law dealt with in the case that relates to headnote 5 of the <u>Thompson</u> v. <u>Economy</u> <u>Super</u> <u>Marts, Inc.</u>, 581 N.Ed.2d 885 (Ill. Ct. App. 1991) case.

2.   Review Illustration 3-6 for questions 2 a-f and 3 through 6.

a.   What is the topic and key number for headnote 3?

b.   What topic would you review in the federal digests to find cases that address points found in the portion of the illustrated case related to headnote 3?

c.   Go to the topic in the federal digest that relates to headnote 3 of Illustration 3-6. What is the first case listed?

d.   Where would you look for the most current case related to this topic in the federal digest? Go there next.

e.   What steps did you take to find the appropriate key number and topic?

f.   What case is the most current case related to that headnote?

3.   For Illustration 3-6, what is the official citation?

4.   For Illustration 3-6, what are the unofficial, parallel citations?

5.   What is the docket number for the case shown in Illustration 3-6?

6.   What judge filed a concurring opinion for the case illustrated in Illustration 3-6?

7.   Review Illustration 3-17. If you were looking for case involving sleeping pills, what topic and key number does this digest page refer you to?

8.   In the digest for your state cases, find the topic hospitals. Review key number 8.

a.   What is the first case listed?

b.   Where is the most current case found?

c.   List the most current case.

9.   Your firm represents a corporation in your state, First Hotels Corporation. It does business in your state. Its headquarters are in your state. Its employees are in your state. It allows a Mexican hotel to use the name First Hotels Corporation. It provides the hotel with some manuals, some suggested rules and some suggested guidelines. When First Hotels Corporation advertises, it agrees based upon the license to include the Mexican First Hotels Corporation in its list of hotels. In the advertisement, First Hotels does not state that it owns or is affiliated with this hotel. The plaintiff, your firm's opponent, injures himself in this Mexican hotel. Assuming the court has jurisdiction in your state and your state law applies, can the plaintiff bring an action against First Hotels Corporation based upon apparent agency?

a.   What is the jurisdiction?

b.   What digest or digests would you use?

c.   Brainstorm. What word or words would you review?

d.   What digest method or methods would you use and why? (List at least two)

e.   List each step you take for each method.

f.   What if any topics would you review?

g.   What key numbers and topics did you find were applicable to this case?

h.   Where did you find the most current cases?

10.   You must determine whether the court is likely to award consequential damages in your case in Indiana. How would you locate case abstracts in the Indiana digest? List at least two methods. Be specific about how you would perform each method and the type of information you would need for each step. Be specific.

a.   If you do not have access to West's Indiana digest, but have access to a computer, first review your state digest. What topic and key number appear to be relevant to this research topic?

b.   Now prepare a computer key number search. List it below.

c.   What service would you use to perform this search?

d.   In what database would you perform this search?

11.   Your firm's client is a 55-year-old man who has a cutlery business in his downtown apartment. Recently an intruder set fire to the apartment building in the apartment just above the client's home. An intruder had been spotted several times by other tenants. The landlord had been notified, but had done nothing to secure the building from the intruder. The client has no insurance and is several months behind in his rent. He has a lot of machinery, an office, clothes, records, knives and other furnishings in his apartment/business. The man living above our client may or may not have insurance. The landlord of the building has insurance for the structure not the individual tenants apartments. The fire may have been caused by the man living above our tenant or by an arsonist. You need to determine whether under any legal theory the landlord could be liable to the tenant in your state.

a.   What is the jurisdiction?

b.   What digest or digests would you use and why?

c.   Brainstorm. What terms would you review?

d.   What digest method or methods would you use and why? (List at least two)

e.   List each step you take for each method.

f.   What if any topics would you review?

g.   What key numbers and topics did you find were applicable to this case?

h.   Where did you find the most current cases?

12.   Review the case found at 704 F.2d 347.

a.   What is the name of the case?

b.   What is the topic and key number listed for headnote 3.

c.   What digest would you look in to find the key number and topic?

d.   Review the topic and key number. List the first two cases found at that topic and key number.

e.   Where would you find the most current cases? List the most current case.

13.   Find the case located at 711 F.2d 1332.

a.   What is the name of this case?

b.   What digest would you review to find the topic and key number for headnote 8?

c.   What is the topic and key number for headnote 8?

d.   Review the appropriate digest and key number. For this problem, you must review the digest carefully if you are using a very current digest. This can be tricky, but will be good practice.

e.   What is the first case listed in the digest?

f.   Where would you find the most current case?

g.   What is the most current case for this key number and topic?

Chapter 4
Shepardizing

Basic Concepts Exercises

1.   What is Key Cite and why would you use it?

2.   What is Auto-Cite?

3.   What is the difference between Shepard's and Auto-Cite?

4.   List three advantage of using Shepard's online?

5.   To thoroughly validate a case, what services should you consult. List all.

6.   If you are Shepardizing a case and you find that it has been overruled, what is your next step? Is there any reason you might rely on this case even though it had been overruled?

7.   For what reasons would you use Shepard's? List at least three reasons.

8.   Why would you use both KeyCite and Shepard's for the same case?

9.   What cases are searched when you use KeyCite?

10.   Who writes the Shepard's treatments?

Application of Shepard's Concepts Exercises

Review Illustration 4-1 and refer to case 582 N.E.2d 125 for questions 1-8.

1.   What is the case name?

2.   What year was the case decided?

3.   What is the parallel citation and how do you know this is the parallel citation?

4.   Assume that this is the only place 582 N.E.2d 125 appears in Shepard's citations, has it been overruled?

5.   What headnotes of 582 N.E.2d 125 are referenced in the cases indicated in this Shepard's notation?

6.   What does the "f" in front of one of the cases mean?

7.   List a U.S. Supreme Court case which cites 582 N.E.2d 125.

8.   List an ALR annotation which cites 582 N.E.2d 125.

9.   Shepardize this case on the computer, if a computer is available to you.

10.   How would you perform a Key Cite of this case on the computer? What service would you use? If this is available to you, perform the Key Cite now.

Chapter 5
Secondary Authority

Basic Concepts Exercises

1. What are the American Law Reports? What is found in the American Law Reports? What is the common abbreviation for the American Law Reports?

2. What are hornbooks?

3. What is a legal encyclopedia? What do you use a legal encyclopedia for when researching?

4. What are the Restatements of the Law?

5. What is secondary authority? Please provide three examples of secondary authority.

6. What is a treatise?

Application of Encyclopedia Concepts

1.   An associate in your department asked you to look up the right of an owner of adjoining property to make improvements on his property when the improvements involved entering the adjoining landowner's property. Sometimes this is classified under adjoining landowners in an encyclopedia.

a.   Use Corpus Juris Secundum to do this problem. First consult the index to find where the right of adjoining landowners to enter neighboring property to make improvements and repairs is mentioned. Where in the index did you find the entry?

b.   What is the index entry?

c.   Find the discussion in <u>C.J.S.</u> that the index led you to. Where is the discussion in <u>C.J.S.</u>?

d.   What is the Bluebook cite?

e.   Read the section that you found in <u>C.J.S.</u> Are you led to any other resources?

f.   Are encyclopedias finding tools and if so, why?

g.   How would you update the <u>C.J.S.</u> section?

2.   An associate in your department asked you to look up the right of an owner of adjoining property to make improvements on his property when the improvements involved entering the adjoining landowner's property. Sometimes this is classified under adjoining landowners in an encyclopedia.

a.   Use <u>American Jurisprudence 2d</u> to do this problem. First consult the index to find where the right of adjoining landowners to enter neighboring property to make improvements and repairs is mentioned. Where in the index did you find the entry. What is the index entry that led you to the discussion?

b.   Find the discussion in <u>Am. Jur. 2d</u> that the index entry led you to. Where is the discussion in <u>Am. Jur. 2d.</u>?

c.   What is the correct Bluebook citation?

d.   Read the section that you found in <u>Am. Jur.</u> Are you led to any other resources?

e.   Are encyclopedia finding tools and if so why?

f.   How would you update the <u>Am. Jur. 2d</u> section?

g.   If you have a cite to an excellent statute that is on point for your research, how would you find references to statutes in <u>Am. Jur. 2d</u>?

Application of Restatements Concepts

1.   Use the <u>Restatement of the Law Second for Agency 2d</u> to answer the following questions.

a.   In general, what are the Restatements?

b.   Use the index to the <u>Restatement of Law Second for Agency 2d</u> to find the section discussing a servant engaging in frolic and detour. Frolic and detour is when an agent or servant is not acting in the scope of his employment and goes off to another area or locality. An example is when Mr. Brand is supposed to deliver a package to the building next door and he goes home for lunch, home is two miles away, before delivering the package. Mr. Brand's eating lunch at home is not within the scope of his employment and constitutes frolic and detour. Under what index heading did you look?

c.   Find the sections in the Restatement and read them. Which section pertains to the question?

d.   What is the complete Bluebook citation for the answer to question c?

2.   Use the <u>Restatement of Law Second for Contracts 2nd</u> to answer the following questions.

a.   In general, what are the Restatements?

b.   Use the index to the <u>Restatement of Law Second for Contracts 2nd</u> to find the section discussing recovery for loss due to emotional disturbance. Under which index heading did you find this information?

c.   What is the section in the <u>Restatement of Law Second for Contracts 2nd</u>?

d.   What is the complete Bluebook citation?

Application of Secondary Authority Research Concepts

1.   This problem requires you to use a variety of secondary sources.

Ms. Smith came to our firm because she wants to know if she should sue an auto body shop for not performing repairs that they claimed to have made. Ms. Smith hit a curb in an ice storm last fall. The left control arm of her car was damaged due to the impact with the curb. Her local service station told her about the problem and recommended that she bring her car, a late model Lunar, to an auto body shop. The car's steering was very imprecise and it was dangerous to drive. She brought the car to Joe's Auto Body where they said yes indeed it is the control arm and they will repair it for $1400. She said okay and they performed the work. Ms. Smith drove the car home and the steering still felt loose. Ms. Smith had to turn the wheel a lot to just make a turn. Ms. Smith drove the car for one week and decided to bring the car back to Joe's. Joe's gave her a 5 year warranty for parts and service. She brought the car in and Joe said that she would have to leave it for an entire day, which she did. She picked up the car and Joe said "the car was perfectly fine" and "anytime you have a day to waste dear we will be glad to look at the car again." Ms. Smith drove the car home and the steering still felt loose. Two weeks later Ms. Smith needed the water pump repaired on the car and brought the car into Lunar Repair. The mechanic hoisted the car up on the lift and said "did you know that your left control arm needs repair?" Ms. Smith had Lunar Repairs write up an estimate with the work that needs to be done in detail. Ms. Smith came to our firm because she feels that she is a victim of fraud.

a.   How would you educate yourself on this topic?

b.   List three secondary sources that you would consult and why you would consult them:

c.   Which source offers the most expansive treatment on the topic of fraud?

Application of A.L.R. Concepts

1.   An associate in your department asked you to look up the right of an owner of adjoining property to make improvements on his property when the improvements involved entering the adjoining landowner's property. Consult the A.L.R. for any relevant annotations.

a.   Use the Quick Index to the A.L.R. 3rd, 4th, and 5th. Under what heading would you look for relevant annotations?

b.   Now use the ALR Index which covers ALR, 2d, 3d, 4th, 5th, Federal and Lawyers Edition and look up relevant annotations. Under what heading would you look for relevant annotations?

c.   What is the difference between the A.L.R. Quick Index and the A.L.R. Index?

d.   Why would you use an A.L.R. annotation for research?

e.   How would you update an annotation?

2.   Partner Jones asked you to find some relevant information on the Consumer Product Safety Act. A little girl was hurt while playing with a toy dart set. She has the text of the statute but needs some secondary authority resources that provide analysis and commentary discussing what is a consumer product for purposes of the act.

a.   Start with the A.L.R. How would you find an A.L.R. annotation on point?

b.   Under which index headings would you search for relevant annotations?

c.   What is a relevant annotation?

d.   What is the complete Bluebook citation for the annotation?

e.   Does the relevant A.L.R. annotation lead you to any other secondary sources?

Application of Legal Periodical Concepts

The following questions require you to use either Current Law Index or Index to Legal Periodicals. If you have access to both indices, you will have the opportunity to compare them.

1.   What time frame is covered in Volume 33 of the Index to Legal Periodicals?

2.   Use the index set that you have at your library and look for an article about the professional athlete's estate planning concepts. Use the volumes mentioned in Question 1 to answer the following:

a.   Under what subject headings did you check?

b.   Under what subject heading is the article listed?

c.   What is the name of the article?

d.   Who is the author?

e.   What is the complete Bluebook citation to the article?

Chapter 6
Constitutions and Statutes

Basic Concepts Exercises

1. What type of authority is a constitution?

2. How does a bill become enacted into law in the United States Congress?

3. What are the Statutes at Large?

4. What is the official version of the federal statutes called?

5. What are the two unofficial versions of the federal statutes?

6. What is the name of your state statutes?

7. Does your state have an unofficial code?

8. Can federal statutes be Shepardized?

9.   Can state statutes be Shepardized?

Application of United States Code Concepts

1.   Use the Popular Name Table of the United States Code 1988 edition, Supplement V 1993, to find the Elementary and Secondary Education Act of 1965. When you use the Popular Name Table of the United States Code, what is the first entry?

2.   Now use the Popular Name Table of the United States Code Annotated and look up the Elementary and Secondary Education Act of 1965. What is the first entry?

3.   What is the difference in the entries in the U.S.C. Popular Name Table and the U.S.C.A.?

4.   How are popular names of acts organized in a Popular Name Table?

5.   What information can you find when looking up an act in a Popular Name Table? Name at least two:

6.   How many titles are there in the United States Code?

7.   What are the unofficial statutory compilations for the United States Code?

8.   Who publishes the unofficial federal codes?

9.   Why is it important to ascertain the publisher of the unofficial code?

10.   Partner Smith as asked you to use the United States Code to find a statute pertaining to the following problem. Mr. Russell McRussell became a partner at his law firm and now must pay for his own health insurance premiums. Mr. McRussell wants to know if the premiums are a deduction for federal tax purposes. You have to go the United States Code and find the pertinent section of the tax code that covers the deduction of health insurance premiums. Use the United States Code Annotated if it is available for this assignment.

a.   Begin with the index. Under which terms did you search for entries regarding the tax aspects of health insurance premiums or costs for self-employed individuals? Please list all of the terms you searched under to find the answer.

b.   Now go to the Code section that you found in the index. Which Code section is it?

c.   Read the Code section and find the subsection pertaining to the problem. Is there anything on point?

d.   Update the Code section by consulting the pocket part. Did you find anything on point?

e.   Does this statute cease to apply after a certain date and if so what is the date?

f.   Shepardize the code section.

Application of Federal Legislative Process Concepts

1.   What are federal slip laws called?

2.   Where do you find federal slip laws?

3.   Where do you find the federal session laws?

4.   How do you determine a United States Code citation if you only have the United States Statutes at Large citation?

5.   How does a bill become law in the federal government?

6.   How do you update a federal statute?

7.   Can you Shepardize a code section?

Application of Updating Concepts: Updating State Statutes using either Computer Assisted Legal Research or Hard Copy Resources

1.   In your state code, look up the law regarding sending unsolicited goods to a consumer. This is generally under the heading of consumer protection. Find the statute section for your state code and then update it by either using LEXIS or WESTLAW.

a.   Which Library and File on LEXIS would you use to find the information? In the alternative, in which database would you find this information on WESTLAW?

b.   How would you update this information on either LEXIS or WESTLAW?

c.   If LEXIS and WESTLAW are not available, how would you update the statutory provision to ensure that it is the most current form of the legislation on point?

Application of State Statutory Research Concepts

1.   In your state code, look up the residency requirement for divorce in your state. How long must a person reside in your state before he or she can file an action for divorce?

a.   Under which index entries did you search?

b.   What is the statute cite in correct Bluebook format?

c.   Did you update your answer? How did you update your answer?

State Statutory Research Exercises

1.   What is the statute of limitations to file an action for assault in your state?

2.   Under which index entries did you search?

3.   What is the statute cite in correct Blubook format?

4.   Did you update your answer? How did you update your answer?

Chapter 7
Legislative History

Application of Legislative History Concepts

1.   What is the source that contains compiled legislative histories of federal law?

2.   Who publishes this source?

3.   This company also publishes one version of the annotated federal statutes, which statute set do they publish?

4.   Why is it important that the same company published the compiled federal legislative histories and the annotated federal statutes?

5.   What is a legislative history and why do we use them?

6.   Partner Smith asked you to find the legislative history of 16 U.S.C. §583d.

a.   How would you find the legislative history of this statute?

b.   How would you cite the statute section?

c.   What is the subject of the statute and the legislative history?

d.   What does the legislative history contain?

e.   What is the correct Bluebook citation to the Senate Report for this Public Law in USCCAN?

7.   You have been asked to find the applicable code sections that contain the federal Wild Bird Conservation Act of 1992 and perform a legislative history of the act.

a.   Where are the sections in the United States Code and how did you find them?

b.   What is the Public Law number for the Wild Bird Conservation Act of 1992?

c.   Please find the legislative history of the Wild Bird Conservation Act of 1992. Where would you find it?

d.   Read the legislative history of the Act. What information is provided and what types of documents are included?

e.   Why is the Public Law different than the codified version of the statute?

Chapter 8
Administrative Materials and Looseleaf Services

Basic Concepts Exercises

1.   What does the Federal Register contain and how often is it published?

2.   What is the CFR?

3.   List three examples of primary authority which might be found in a looseleaf?

4.   A looseleaf service:

   a. is comprehensive
   b. is current
   c. is a mini-library
   d. contains only commentary
   e. a, b and c only
   f. a-d above

5.   Looseleaf services often contain:

   a. commentary written by attorneys
   b. commentary written by publishers
   c. primary authorities
   d. a and c only
   e. b and c only
   f. a-c above

6.   What are the functions of an administrative agency?

7.   Can an administrative agency hold hearings?

8.   What type of authority do administrative agencies generate?

9.   What is an enabling statute?

10.   What is the difference between the C.F.R. and the Federal Register?

Application of Administrative Law Concepts Exercises

Note: The answers to the questions concerning the regulations will vary depending upon the year in which these exercises are completed.

1.   Find the Federal Register for March 1, 1995. Find a final rule that deals with the standards and grades for colby cheese.

a.   What is the effective date of the new rule?

b.   What is the federal register citation?

c.   What C.F.R. part does this rule affect?

d.   Provide the Federal Register citation in proper Bluebook format.

2.   Now review the Federal Register for March 30, 1995. Use the L.S.A. to update the C.F.R. part affected by the final rule noted in question 5 below. What does it tell you?

3.   Find 60 F.R. 10304.

a.   What is the subject of this Federal Register page?

b.   Who should you contact for more information about this subject?

c.   What C.F.R. sections are affected by this Federal Register section?

d.   What is the statutory authority for 39 C.F.R. part 381 mentioned in this section?

4.   Find 7 C.F.R. 58.2826.

a.   What is the topic of this regulation?

b.   What Federal Register citations are provided for this regulation's history section?

c.   Provide the proper Bluebook citation for this regulation.

5.   Find 9 C.F.R. 317.313.

a.   What is the topic of this regulation?

b.   What Federal Register citations are provided for this regulation's history section?

c.   What other C.F.R. parts must be read to fully understand this regulation?

d.   Provide the proper Bluebook citation for this regulation.

6.   What regulation specifies the requirements for claims made concerning "Percent fat free?" How did you find this regulation? List the steps you took.

7.   Find 49 C.F.R. 571.213.

a.   What is the topic of this regulation?

b.   What is the scope of the regulation?

c.   What is the purpose of the regulation?

d.   What telephone number does the regulation provide for information about product recalls?

e.   Look in the List of Affected Sections and determine whether this regulation has been amended, changed, updated or removed.

8.   Using the current Federal Register index, determine if any new regulations have been adopted concerning the topic of the regulation found in question 7. What words did you use to consult the index?

9.   Use the Internet to find regulations concerning small parts in children's toys.

        a.   What is the citation in Bluebook format.

        b.   Go to Federal Register section noted.

        c.   What do you learn about who to contact concerning this regulation?

10.   Use the Internet to find a regulation that concerns airbags in passenger cars. Note the citation.

Chapter 9
Computerized Legal Research

Basic Concepts Exercises

1.   What are connectors? What are the LEXIS connectors? What are the WESTLAW connectors?

2.   What is WIN on WESTLAW?

3.   What is LEXIS Freestyle?

4.   How is information organized on LEXIS?

5.   How is information organized on WESTLAW?

6.   What is a search query?

7.   What is in the LEXIS News Library?

8.   What is Keycite on WESTLAW?

Application Exercises

Is the Torrens system of registering title to real property adopted in your state? If the Torrens system is adopted in your state find the pertinent statute section from your state code and find a case from your state's supreme court discussing the Torrens system.

a.   How would you compose the query when searching for the statute section on WESTLAW? What database would you select?

b.   How would you compose the query when searching for the statute section on LEXIS? What Library and file would you select?

c.   What is the search term or key word that would appear in a document on point?

d.   How would you compose the query when searching for a state supreme court case discussing the Torrens system on LEXIS? Print out the citation to the most recent case that you found.

e.   How would you compose the query when searching for a state supreme court case discussing the Torrens system on WESTLAW? Print out the citation to the most recent case that you found.

f.   If you have LEXIS available, Shepardize the citation that you used in question d. Update the Shepard's information with LexCite. Print out this information.

g.   If you have WESTLAW available, KeyCite the citation that you used in question e. Print out this information.

2.   Robert and Jan Moore live in Evingston, Anywhere and are building an addition and repairing the gutters on their house on Ashville Street. There is eight feet between their house and the house belonging to Mrs. Jones, their neighbor. There is no alley on the back and no driveway that goes to their house. The property is adjoining. The Moores' contractors and construction workers must enter the neighbor's property, Mrs. Jones', to the north, to perform their work. Mrs. Jones is not very pleased that the workers are entering her property. Mrs. Jones may be induced to permit the work if the Moores obtain a license from her. The Moores came to us to find out what is entailed in obtaining a license.

The two issues to focus on are what is a license in your jurisdiction and is granting a license controlled by a statute or case law in your jurisdiction.

a.   How would you compose the query when searching for the statute section on WESTLAW? What database would you select?

b.   How would you compose the query when searching for the statute section on LEXIS? What Library and file would you select?

c.   What is the search term or key word that would appear in a document on point?

d.   How would you compose the query, on LEXIS, when searching for a state supreme court case discussing granting or obtaining a license to use the property of another? This case should contain the general rule or elements of obtaining or granting a license in your jurisdiction. Print out the citation to the most recent case that you found.

e.   How would you compose the query, on WESTLAW, when searching for a state supreme court case discussing granting or obtaining a license to use the property of another? This case should contain the general rule or elements of obtaining or granting a license in your jurisdiction. Print out the citation to the most recent case that you found.

f.   If you have LEXIS available, Shepardize the citation that you used in question d. Update the Shepard's information with LexCite. Print out this information.

g.   If you have WESTLAW available, KeyCite the citation that you used in question e. Print out this information.

Application of Advanced Computerized Legal Research Concepts

1.   Mr. Michael Jones came to our firm with the following problem. Jones purchased a tractor-trailer rig on November 28, 1994 from Grimy Auto and Truck. Grimy is a dealer in used trucks that buys, reconditions and sells trucks. The purchase agreement was based on the following conditions: the engine was to be overhauled using rebuilt and reconditioned parts; the parts were to be guaranteed and invoices provided; the truck was to be ready to use in the manner consistent with the type of work Jones needed it for - long haul trucking or over-the-road interstate trucking. Jones paid in full for the truck. The truck was found to have some old parts as well as some defective ones. Consequently, the truck repeatedly broke down causing Mr. Jones to miss jobs for

long periods of time. Jones lost wages as a result. Jones was also forced to make extensive repairs to the truck. In May and June of 1995, Jones made three repairs totalling $4163.67. The truck is currently disabled with estimated repair costs of $9000. Jones wishes to pursue damages for breach of contract against Grimy.

Focus your research on the following issues: What constitutes effective rejection of defective goods in your jurisdiction? What constitutes acceptance of non-conforming goods in your jurisdiction?

a.   Compose a query that you would use on LEXIS to search for two state supreme court decision articulating the general rules relating to the issues. What is the query? What are the state supreme court cases? Print the cases in KWIC format.

b.   Compose a query that you would use on WESTLAW to search for two state supreme court decisions articulating the general rules relating to the issues. What is the query? What are the state supreme court cases? Print the cases in Term mode.

c.   If you are using LEXIS, Shepardize and LexCite the relevant cases that you found and print out the results.

d.   If you are using WESTLAW, use KeyCite to validate the relevant cases that you found. Please print out the results.

Application of Computerized Factual Research Concepts

1.   The corporate and securities department at your firm needs to produce a newsletter. You have been asked to find articles discussing financial instruments called derivatives. The articles must be timely so you will want articles that are from the past two months only.

a.   If you are using LEXIS to find the articles, in which Library and file would you search?

b.   If you are using WESTLAW to find articles, in which database would you search?

c.   What is your search query on LEXIS?

d.   What is your search query on WESTLAW?

e.   Print out your results in cite format only.

Chapter 10
Internet Research

Basic Concepts Exercises

1.   What is a search engine?

2.   What is a URL?

3.   What is a home page?

4.   What are chat groups?

5.   What types of information can you find on the Internet?

6.   What types of legal information can you find on the Internet?

7.   Can you use the legal sources you find on the Internet as primary official resources?

Application of Concepts

1.   Find two sites that discuss law firms and internet connections.

2.   Find two sites of interest to paralegals.

3.   Note a search engine. Describe how you would use it.

4.   Find two law firm home pages.

Chapter 11
Practice Rules

Basic Concepts Exercises

1.   Do the Federal Rules of Civil Procedure govern a proceeding in your state court?

2.   What type of authority are the Federal Rules of Civil Procedure?

3.   Do the state rules of procedure for your state govern trials in the federal courts located in your state?

4.   What type of authority are your state rules of procedure?

5.   Do the Federal Rules of Evidence apply in proceedings in the federal courts of your state?

6.   Do the Federal Rules of Evidence apply in proceedings in the state courts in your state?

7.   What type of authority are the Federal Rules of Evidence?

8.   Can you Shepardize a Federal Rule of Civil Procedure?

9.   Can you Shepardize a state procedural rule?

10.   List one attorney desk book used in your state.

Application of Concepts Exercises for the Practice Rules

1.   Find a federal rule that explains how to serve a pleading. What is the rule and where did you locate it?

2.   Find a case that explains the rule that is the answer to question 1. Attach a copy of the case to this exercise. What sources did you review to find the case?

3.   Find a local rule for the federal court in your area that deals with the question of the size of the paper that may be filed with the court. What sources did you consult to find this rule?

4.   Find a U.S. Supreme Court rule that deals with the requirements an attorney must meet before he or she can appear before the U.S. Supreme Court. What is the rule number and where did you locate it?

5.   Find a federal rule of evidence that explains the methods for proving character. What is the rule and where did you locate it?

6.   Find the advisory committee notes for the federal rule of evidence 406. In what source did you find these comments? What type of authority are these comments?

7.   Does your state have an evidence code? How would you determine this fact? List two methods and why you would consult that source.

8.   Find a local rule for your federal district court that deals with the question of attorney admission requirements. What is the rule and what are the requirements? Where did you find this information?

9.   Find a federal appellate rule that deals with the issue of the composition of the record on appeal and transcript questions. What is the rule and where did you find it?

10.   Assume you are a paralegal for a firm involved in a products liability action. The plaintiffs, G.I. Fore and M.R. Gott, filed the action against the defendants, William Right and Sy R. Leaf, car manufacturers, in the U.S. District Court for the Northern District of Illinois in Chicago. The plaintiffs were riding in a car. They claim that the car was defective because it was not equipped with air bags. Plaintiffs want to amend their complaint and add another theory of liability against the defendants. Plaintiffs never raised this new theory before this date.

The suit was first brought in the Illinois Circuit Court of Cook County, but was later removed to federal court.

On June 10, 1997, the clerk of the United States District Court sent the plaintiffs attorney, Ira B. Adly a letter. In the letter, the court asked the counsel to enter an appearance in the federal court pursuant to Local Rule 3.14 of the United States District Court for the Northern District of Illinois Eastern Division. This information is contained in a certified copy of the docket sheet.

The plaintiff's counsel later admitted that he was aware that the action was removed to federal court. That admission is contained in a transcript of a May 24, 1999 court hearing and in the plaintiff's motion to vacate judgment. Adly sent several letters to defense counsel which reference the federal court number and the fact that the case was pending in federal court.

The plaintiff's attorney didn't attend four court-set status hearings and failed to appear for a hearing in court. That hearing concerned the defendant's motion to compel. The plaintiffs contend that their attorney never received notice of the status hearings. However, the defendants' attorney, Hal S. Ville, sent copies of the motion to compel to Adly's correct address.

In a conversation with the defense counsel during a deposition and in subsequent letters, defense counsel told the plaintiffs' counsel that a response to this motion was due. Adly never filed a response. Then the defendants' attorney filed a motion for summary judgment and sent a copy to the plaintiffs' counsel at the correct address. Plaintiffs' attorney never answered this motion or another other motion. Adly never filed any motions to extend time.

Adly admitted that he did not call the court to find out why it had not had routine status conferences. The court always holds status conferences regularly.

Because Adly failed to attend any court hearings and failed to file any answers to motions or to appear in this case, the court dismissed the case for failure to prosecute in June 1998. One month later in July of 1998, Adly filed a motion to vacate judgment on behalf of the plaintiffs. The plaintiff did not cite a rule in their motion.

a.   Under what rule are the plaintiffs probably seeking to vacate the judgment?

b.   Where would you find this rule? List three sources.

c.   Where would you find cases that construe this rule? List four sources. Why would you consult a particular source?

You also want to review the local Illinois district court rule. List three sources that might contain this rule whether or not these sources are available to you in your state.

11.   Find the Federal Rules of Procedure on the Internet. List the URL or gopher site.

Basic Concepts Exercises

1.   Do the ethical rules that govern lawyers also apply to paralegals?

2.   What type of authority are ethical rules adopted by your state for attorneys?

3.   What type of authority are the ethical codes and rules prepared by the American Bar Association?

4.   Does one ethics code apply to all of the attorneys in the United States?

5.   Where would you find ethical rules? List two sources.

6.   List two sources that would contain case citations for ethical rules. Why would you use each source.

7.   What type of authority is an ABA ethics opinion?

8.   What type of authority is a decision of your state's highest court concerning an ethics issues?

9.   What secondary sources might be considered to understand ethics topics? List two sources. Explain when and why you would use them.

10.   What is the name of the ethics code for lawyers in your state?

Application of Concept Exercises for the Rules

1.   Find the ABA Model Rule that defines the unauthorized practice of law. What is the rule number and where did you locate it?

2.   What type of authority is the ABA model rule noted in question No.1.

3.   Find the ABA Model Rule that explains a lawyer's responsibilities regarding a nonlawyer assistant. What is the rule number? Where did you find this listed?

4.   Find the rule in your state that relates to the unauthorized practice of law. What is the rule number?

5.   Determine whether there is a rule in your state that is similar to the ABA rule concerning nonlawyer assistants.

6.   Determine whether your state has an ethics rule concerning conflicts of interest between an attorney and a former client. If there is a rule, what is the number of the rule. Where did you find this information.

7.   What sources would you consult to find any cases for your state which deal with the unauthorized practice of law? List two sources, including one source that also would specify any rule concerning the unauthorized practice of law.

8.   What sources would you consult to find any cases for your state which deal with the question of a lawyer's responsibility for his/her nonlawyer assistant?

9.   Find the ABA Ethics opinion, ABA Comm. on Ethics and Professional Responsibility, Informal Op. 1185 (1971) in hardcopy or on the computer. What does this opinion concern?

10.   Find the ABA Ethics opinion, ABA Comm. on Ethics and Professional Responsibility, Informal Op. 1527 (1989). Where did you find this opinion? What does it concern? What type of authority is this opinion?

11.   Find two sites on the Internet that either list ethics rules for lawyers or ethics opinions.

Chapter 13
Practitioner's Materials

Basic Concepts Exercises

1.   Who compiles formbooks?

2.   What type of authority are the forms contained in formbooks?

3.   Who drafts continuing legal education materials?

4.   What type of authority are continuing legal education materials?

5.   What are pattern jury instructions and when would you use them?

6.   Do the federal courts use pattern jury instructions?

7.   What is the name of a law directory that lists lawyers in your state or city?

8.   List three facts you can learn about a lawyer listed in the Martindale-Hubbell Law Directory.

9.   How would you determine whether your state has pattern jury instructions? List two methods.

10.   Are jury instructions available online?

Application of Concepts Exercises for the Practitioner's Materials

1.   Find a sample of corporate bylaws in your state in a state formbook.

2.   Find a sample articles of incorporation for a corporation in your state. List the formbook from your state that you used.

3.   Find a sample will from a continuing legal education guide in your state.

4.   Find a sample trust agreement for your state. What book did you review and why?

5.   Find a jury instruction for your state that defines the functions of the court and the jury.

6.   Find a jury instruction typically given in federal court concerning the functions of the court and the jury.

7.   Find the federal jury instruction that details the standard of proof for the plaintiff in a retaliatory discharge case.

8.   Using the Martindale-Hubbell Law Directory, find the law firm of Sidley & Austin in Chicago, Illinois.

a.   List the steps you took to find it.

b.   What is the address?

c.   What law schools did some of the partners listed attend?

d.   What is the e-mail address for the firm?

9.   Now turn to the front section the Martindale-Hubbell directory, and find attorney Phillip H. Corboy. What is the name of his law firm?

10.   Using the Internet, search for a directory of lawyers.

Chapter 14
Research Strategy

Application of Concepts: Defining the Issues and Determining the Area of Law

1.   Partner Harry Harold asked you to research the following fact pattern based on the law of your jurisdiction.

Robert and Jan Moore live in Evingston, Anywhere and are building an addition and repairing the gutters on their house on Ashville Street. There is eight feet between their house and the house belonging to Mrs. Jones, their neighbor. There is no alley on the back and no driveway that goes to their house. The property is adjoining. The Moores' contractors and construction workers must enter the neighbor's property, Mrs. Jones', to the north, to perform their work. Mrs. Jones is not very pleased that the workers are entering her property. Mrs. Jones may be induced to permit the work if the Moores obtain a license from her. The Moores came to us to find out what is entailed in obtaining a license.

a.   What is the legal issue?

b.   What is the area of law that you would explore?

c.   What sources did you consult and why did you consult them to ascertain the legal issue and the area of law? Name three.

d.   If LEXIS or WESTLAW is available, what would be your query?

2.   Use the facts in question number 1, but now take the time to **diagram** the research process, using hard copy resources.

3.   Diagram the research process using a **combination** of hard copy and computerized resources.

4.   Mr. Michael Jones came to our firm with the following problem:

Jones purchased a tractor-trailer rig on November 28, 1994 from Grimy Auto and Truck. Grimy is a dealer in used trucks that buys, reconditions and sells trucks. The purchase agreement was based on the following conditions: the engine was to be overhauled using rebuilt and reconditioned parts; the parts were to be guaranteed and invoices provided; the truck was to be ready to use in the manner consistent with the type of work Jones needed it for - long haul trucking or over-the-road interstate trucking. Jones paid in full for the truck. The truck was found to have some old parts as well as some defective ones. Consequently, the truck repeatedly broke down causing Mr. Jones to miss jobs for long periods of time. Jones lost wages as a result. Jones was also forced to make extensive repairs to the truck. In May and June of 1995, Jones made three repairs totalling $4163.67. the truck is currently disabled with estimated repair costs of $9000. Jones wishes to pursue damages for breach of contract against Grimy.

a.   What are the legal issues?

b.   What is the area of law that you would explore?

c.   What sources did you consult and why did you consult them to ascertain the legal issue and the area of law? Name three.

d.   If LEXIS or WESTLAW is available, what would be your query?

5.   Using the same set of facts, now take the time to **diagram** the research process, using hard copy resources.

6.   Diagram the research process using a **combination** of hard copy and computerized resources.

Diagram the entire research process that you would follow to resolve the following questions. Use either hard copy resources or a combination of hard copy and computerized resources.

7.   What is the Torrens system.

8.   Is the Torrens system of registering title to real property adopted in your state?

9.   Diagram the entire research process that you would follow to resolve the following question. Use either hard copy resources or a combination of hard copy or computerized resources.

What is your state's law regarding companies sending unsolicited goods to a consumer. This sometimes occurs with book clubs and subscriptions when you join initially you receive a book that you did not order. Be sure that your answer includes validating, Shepardizing, and updating your resources. Answers will vary according to jurisdiction.

10.   You are a paralegal with the Law Office of Warren T. Sales. You have been asked to research the following questions and provide answers. These are the facts that Mr. Sales presented to you.

Your client is Sue A. Seller. She lives at 3225 Wilmette Avenue, Glenview, Your state. The defendants are Lee R. Merchant, owner of Mowers R Us, in Glenview, Your state, and Manny U. Facture, the owner of a manufacturing concern which is not incorporated called Mowers, of Rosemont, Your state. Ms. Seller went to the defendant's store, Mowers R Us, to purchase a lawnmower for her new home. She was a first-time homeowner. She was unfamiliar with lawnmowers. She had never operated a lawnmower because her brothers always had mowed the lawn when she was a child.

When she went to Mowers R Us, she asked to speak with the owner. "I want to speak only to the owner," she told Mr. Merchant. "I don't know anything about these mowers and I need to talk with an expert." Mr. Merchant said, "I'm the owner and you couldn't find a better expert anywhere in the Chicagoland area. I have been in the business of selling mowers for more than 40 years. I only sell mowers and the equipment to clean and repair them. Are you familiar with the type of lawnmower you would like?," Mr. Merchant added.

"No, I don't know anything about lawnmowers. I just know that I have to have a lawnmower that will mulch my grass clippings because I cannot bag the clippings. The village of Glenview does not permit me to bag the clippings. So the clippings must remain on my lawn," Ms. Seller told Mr. Merchant.

"You're absolutely correct. You must have a mulching mower," Mr. Merchant said. "That type of mower will grind the grass clippings and you will not notice them on your grass."

"I have the perfect mower for you," Mr. Merchant continued. "It is a used model that will fit into your price range. It is only $200. It is a good brand a Roro. It will mulch the grass as well as any of the new mowers. This one is true blue. You can purchase a separate mulching blade which will easily attach to it for an additional $50," he added.

"Do you think that I need the mulching blade," Ms. Seller asked, "I've never used a lawnmower so I don't know what to expect and you appear to be the expert."

"I think that you could do without the mulching blade unless you want the grass ground up very fine," Mr. Merchant said.

"I think that I would like it ground up fine. I'll defer to your judgment. If you think a mulching blade is necessary, then I'll buy that with the mower. Do you think that this is the best mower for mulching?," asked Ms. Seller.

"Absolutely, I told you it is a true value. It will mulch with the best of them," Mr. Merchant said.

"If you think it can do the job, I'll trust your judgment," said Ms. Seller. "I'll take the mower and the mulching blade. Can you install the mulching blade. I don't know anything about the installation."

"Sure, we can install any blade for another $30.00," Mr. Merchant said.

"OK. Do you clean up the machine, too?," Ms. Seller asked.

"We can do it for an additional $40 or you can do it yourself with the special industrial strength, non-toxic, non-irritant mower cleaner," Mr. Merchant told Ms. Seller.

"Well I have sensitive skin, do you really think that the mower cleaner is safe for me to use? I have never used any type of industrial strength cleaner, Ms. Seller said.

"Absolutely, I've used the cleaner many times and it is very safe and won't hurt your sensitive skin at all."

Ms. Seller purchased the mower, the blade and the cleaner. She used the mower after Mr. Merchant installed the new mulching blade. It barely cut the grass and certainly didn't mulch the clippings into fine pieces as Mr. Merchant had claimed.

She brought the mower back to Mr. Merchant. He said that he had made no warranties about the mower. He showed her the language on the receipt which said that he did not expressly warrant anything.

Ms. Seller brought the mower to a Roro dealer. The owners of the Roro dealership, Abe Saul and Lou T. Wright, said that the mower Ms. Seller had purchased from Mowers R Us was not a mulching mower. It was a mower built before mulching was popular. Therefore, it would not perform the mulching task. It was designed merely to cut the grass. "Any merchant who has been in business for one year or more should have known that mowers built before 1970 were not designed for mulching," Mr. Wright said. He showed Ms. Seller where the manufacturing date appeared on the mower. "Manufactured in August 1969," it said on the plate with the serial number. "Also, mulching blades cannot be placed on these old mowers. Any mower dealer should know that too," Mr. Wright added. "However, this mower isn't defective. It can cut the grass without mulching it."

The mower wasn't Ms. Seller's only problem. She also had used the cleaner with gloves. She broke out in rash all over her hands. The dermatologist stated that the cleaner was caustic and permeated the gloves, causing the rash on Ms. Seller's hands.

Ms. Seller is bringing an action against Mr. Merchant and Mr. Facture in the Circuit Court of Cook County, Law Division in Your state. Your research is limited to actions Ms. Seller has against Mr. Merchant for breach of an implied warranty of fitness for a particular purpose. Only answer the questions below.

Answer each of the following questions fully and provide authority i.e., cases, secondary sources, if necessary, or laws, to support your position. Indicate whether the authority is primary or secondary authority and whether it is mandatory or persuasive authority. Remember that your goal is to find the best primary binding authorities.

a.	First, what law of what jurisdiction governs this problem and what is the highest court in the jurisdiction?

b.	Where should you begin your research? List any sources you plan to consult. Indicate whether the sources contain primary or secondary sources. List any finding tools you plan to use. Explain why you plan to use each source.

c.	List any secondary and primary sources you consulted. List the sources in order of your consultation. List any finding tools you used. Indicate where you located information in these references.

d.　　Based on your research in this jurisdiction, can Ms. Seller sue Mr. Merchant for breach of an implied warranty of fitness for a particular purpose with regard to the lawnmower purchase? (Please provide any authority which supports your position. Use Bluebook format.　If necessary, attach additional pages. Write the holding for each authority or a basic summary of the value of that authority. Indicate whether the authority is primary or secondary and whether it is binding.

e.　　Based upon the law of this jurisdiction, is Mr. Merchant a merchant?　(Please provide any authority which supports your position. Please use Bluebook format. If necessary, attach additional pages. Write the holding for each authority or a basic summary of the value of that authority. Indicate whether the authority is primary or secondary and whether it is binding.)

f.　　If Ms. Seller is entitled to recovery of damages for breach of an implied warrant of fitness for a particular purpose in this jurisdiction, does the fact that the mower was a "used product" prohibit Ms. Seller's recovery?　(Please provide any authority which supports your position. Please use Bluebook format. If necessary, attach additional pages. Write the holding for each authority or a basic summary of the value of that authority. Indicate whether the authority is primary or secondary and whether it is binding.)

g.　　If Ms. Seller is entitled to recovery of damages for breach of an implied warrant of fitness for a particular purpose does the fact that the mower was not defective prohibit her recovery? (Please provide any authority that supports your position. Please use Bluebook format. If necessary, attach additional pages. Write the holding for each authority or a basic summary of the value of that authority. Indicate whether the authority is primary or secondary and whether it is binding.)

h.　　Does Ms. Seller have a cause of action for breach of an implied warranty of fitness for a particular purpose with regard to the cleaner? (Please provide any authority which supports your position. Please use Bluebook format.　If necessary, attach additional pages. Write the holding for each authority or a basic summary of the value of that authority. Indicate whether the authority is primary or secondary and whether it is binding.)

i.　　After you have found the authorities in the print materials, use the appropriate computer database or databases to augment your search. What searches would be helpful? Formulate them before you approach the computer. List them below.

j.   Validate your research authorities on the computer as described above. Attach the cite checking results. Also use LEXIS as a citator to retrieve cases after 1960.

Chapter 15
Getting Ready to Write

Exercises

1.   Use a paper that you have written for this exercise.

a.   Examine the paper – What is the purpose and the audience?

b.   Extract an outline from the paper – outline the ideas explained in the paper.

c.   Revise your outline to clarify your ideas.

2.   Write a letter to a neighbor discussing the highlights of the past season.

a.   What is the audience and, consequently, the tone?

b.   Rewrite the letter to a government official. In the rewritten letter, express dissatisfaction with a service that is supposed to be provided by the local government and was not provided adequately during the past season. For example, in the letter to your neighbor, you write about the great snowfall during the winter. In the rewritten letter to a government official, you also write about the great snowfall, but also include how the locality failed to plow sufficiently. What is the purpose and audience of the letter to the government official?

Application of Concepts Exercises

Please correct the grammar if necessary. Make the sentences more concise.

1. The police report said that Mr. Harris had a blood alcohol level of 1.7 based on an on-site blood alcohol test and states further that there were swerve marks on the street. The report also stated that there were no brake marks and that the officer cites the driver for drunk driving.

2. The personnel manager did all of the hiring and firing of the restaurant and golf course and the part-time accountant manages all bookkeeping and tax work for the restaurant and golf course.

3. Candy Graham who did not have an employment contract was, despite her freedom to set her own hours and work from her own home, an employee.

4. Janice was told she was suffering from shock after an examination at the time of the accident by her son's physician.

5. The court believes that the plaintiff should prove all elements of negligence before the defendant will be held liable.

Tightening Exercises

1.   At approximately 7:30 p.m. on May 4, 1998, the plaintiff, Linda Gregory, was weeding the front garden at her home at 2099 Vista Drive in Phoenix. She was about five feet from the street. The children also were playing in the front yard which was near the street.

2.   Based on a blood-alcohol test done at the scene of the accident, it was determined that Ronnie Walden was intoxicated.

3.   As a result, Walden was given a citation for driving while intoxicated and reckless operation of a motor vehicle.

4.   The tort for which Ms. Cannon is suing arises from Ms. Cannon's observation of her son on the ground covered with blood and blood all over Mr. Connelley's Cadillac which has caused her to have nightmares, sleepless nights and problems eating.

5.   When Wright bought the land, he was aware that a funeral home and a combination horse farm/dog kennel were in operation just outside of the subdivision.

6.   The day the accident occurred it was very clear and had not rained to make the road slick.

7.   If our clients' interest in their land is substantially invaded by stables or kennel as a result of odors and sounds created by the proper conduct of those businesses and not taking into account any special sensitivities on the part of our clients, is the harm to our clients significantly more important than the benefit of the stables or kennel to the community?

8.   The issue is whether or not it is a nuisance.

9.   In considering whether Kurth is an employee or an independent contractor, she is probably considered to be an employee.

Screening for Legalese: Say it in English, Please.

1.   In the aforementioned case, the funeral home was not found to be a nuisance because the court held that the funeral home in question was "reasonably located on the outskirts of the city."

2.   Plaintiff was weeding her garden which is in front of her house, but not in clear view from said house.

3.   Now comes the plaintiff, by and through her attorney, causes this complaint to be filed with the court.

4.   Further affiant sayest not.

5.   The party of the first part claims that the party of the second part said that he wanted to cause her to go out of business.

6.   The Whole In One , hereinafter referred to as WIO , is a subsidiary of Good Ole Times Enterprises.

Active and Passive Exercises

1.   Two businesses are owned by Ned and Wally Maine and they are being sued in federal court by two former workers for sex discrimination.

2.   Eve Kurth was paid by the Maines on commission. She was paid bi-weekly.

3.   Cammy Ashton's office supplies and office were provided by Whole In One .

4.   Bonnie Bill was let into the building by a security guard who thought she wanted to look for lost jewelry.

5.   Ronnie's blood alcohol level was tested by the police and found to be 1.1.

6.   In Consolidation, the court was urged to abandon this test, which was rejected by the U.S. Supreme Court.

7.   The funeral home was controlled by William Halsey and owned jointly by Halsey and Victor Phillip.

Application of Concepts Exercises for Grammar Tips

Please correct the grammar if necessary. Make the sentences more concise.

1.   To receive this protection in the corporate setting, an individual must show that they were a decision-making employee of the corporation at the time such communications for which the privilege is asserted were made.

2.   The threshold element to address in determining employee protection under the attorney-client privilege is whether he was employed at the time the conversations for which the privilege is being asserted were held.

3.   The extent of the employer's control and supervision over the worker, including directions on scheduling and performance of work.

4.   Janice, at the time of the accident, was unable to move, believed at first that her son was dead.

5.   An individual is considered an employee under Title VII when they are titled a sales representative, provide regular sales reporters, are reimbursed for some business expenses, can draw against their commission, and has taxes withheld by the employer.

6.   She alleges in her deposition that the defendant was driving recklessly and with intention struck her son with his car.

7.   Plaintiff believes, despite defendant's remarks, that the driver intentionally hit her son to cause her distress, although Ronnie has never threatened her in the past.

8.   Plaintiffs probably will not succeed in vacating the judgment of June 1989 because relief from judgment is an extraordinary remedy granted in exceptional circumstances, and the facts of this case only show Adly's inexcusable neglect under no extraordinary circumstances.

9.   Whether the only funeral home in the area, operating since the 1940s, is a nuisance under common law?

10.   This case is similar because the farm was established before the development of the subdivision and the resort, so it could be assumed that the horse breeding farm is a useful enterprise.

11.   Ashton worked without supervision from the company offices.

12.   Mrs. Gerphart, at first thought her son, Patrick, was dead because of the amount of blood and broken bones that surrounded the car.

13.   Patrick cannot play t-ball for the rest of the season and he and his family cannot attend their family vacation to the Wisconsin Dells due to Patrick's injuries.

14.   The Whole In One want to show that they are a company who hired these women as independent contractors not employees.

Chapter 18
Briefing Cases

Basic Concepts Exercises

1.   List two reasons to brief a case.

2.   List two essential items that should be noted in the case brief.

3.   What is the procedural history?

4.   What are the issues?

5.   What is the holding?

6.   What are relevant facts?

7.   What is dicta and why would you include it in a brief?

8.   What is the case's disposition?

9.   What is the case's rationale?

10.   Who is the brief generally designed to assist?

Application of Briefing Concepts Exercises

For the following exercises, please review the case of <u>Hornick</u> v. <u>Borough</u> of <u>Duryea</u>, 507 F. Supp. 1091 (1980).

1. Which is the best issue statement concerning the part-time employees concerns in the <u>Hornick</u> case?

a.   Whether part-time workers who are hired, controlled and paid by a company are counted one of a company's 15 employees under Title VII, even though they work only a few hours a day.

b.   Whether the defendant had at least 15 employees to be considered an employer for Title VII purposes. Subissue: Whether part-time workers were to be counted as employees in determining if a person is an employer under Title VII.

c.   Whether the plaintiff was discriminated against solely because of her sex based on a height and weight requirement according to the theory of disparate treatment and disparate impact?

d.   Whether part-time workers who only work a couple of hours a day are considered employees for Title VII purposes?

2. Read the following statements. Which is the best holding and why?

a.   Yes. Even though they work only few hours a day, part-time workers are counted as one of the 15 employees required for Title VII application, when they are hired, controlled and paid by a company.

b.   Yes. The defendant had at least 15 employees and therefore, was subject to Title VII coverage. Subissue: Yes. Part-time workers are to be counted as employees to determine if a person is an employer for Title VII purposes.

c.   According to disparate impact theory and disparate treatment theory plaintiff was discriminated against solely based on a discriminatory height and weight requirement.

d.   The court found that it was not significant that the worker only worked a couple of hours a day with minimal pay. These workers were hired, controlled and paid by the Borough and were therefore considered "employees" for Title VII purposes.

e.   The court held that the non-CETA full and part-time employees exceeded the jurisdictional requirement of Title VII.

Briefing Exercises

1.   Create your own brief for question involving part-time employees and coverage under Title VII presented in Hornick v. Borough of Duryea, 507 F. Supp. 1091 (1980).

2.   Find Barrett Indus. Trucks v. Old Republic Ins., 129 F.R.D. 515 (N.D. Ill. 1990). Brief this case.

3.   Find Spirides v. Reinhardt, 486 F. Supp. 685 (D.C. 1980). Brief this case.

Chapter 19
The Legal Memorandum

Basic Concepts Exercises

1. What is the purpose of an office memorandum?

2. Who is the audience of the memorandum?

3. Should an office memorandum be one-sided and persuasive in nature?

4. What is the purpose of a conclusion?

5. What facts should be included in the facts statement?

6. Should the discussion section provide a history of the applicable law?

Chapter 20
Questions Presented or Issues *and* Conclusions or Brief Answers

Issue Exercises: What is missing?

1. Were the Maines, owners of Whole In One , an employer under federal law?

2. Was Eve Kurth an employee under federal law?

Issue Drafting Exercise

1.   You are a paralegal with the firm of Probing and Will. You must research whether Sarah Wakefield can renounce Adam Antwernts' will and collect a portion of the estate.

Your firm's client is Sarah Wakefield. She was married to Adam Antwernt. Antwernt died on June 6, 1998 in your state following a long illness. Wakefield was Antwernt's second wife. She had been married to him for more than 20 years and lived in their home in the Highlands of your state. Antwernt purchased the home with his first wife, Carry MacOver. MacOver died in 1965. When Antwernt married Wakefield he never changed the deed for the home to include Wakefield. Wakefield kept her maiden name. Antwernt adopted a son with MacOver in 1964. The son, who is now 30 years old is Grayson Antwernt.

Antwernt drafted his will in May of 1992. He and his wife were getting along fine. However, he excluded her from his will. He did not leave her any property. Instead, he left all of his property to Grayson. Antwernt's will was admitted to probate on July 8, 1998.

Wakefield wants to know whether Antwernt's will is valid and whether he can divest her of the marital property or whether she can renounce the will and collect a portion of the estate.

Grayson is out of town and his attorney told Wakefield that she will get her share of the estate once Grayson returns. He is scheduled to return on July 5, 1999.

Please prepare an issue statement for this problem.

2.   Review the following facts. Then prepare an issue statement for this problem.

Your client, Hospitality Resorts International, Inc., which does business in your state is defending an action against James Panhandle, a 70-year-old doctor from Akron, Ohio, who slipped and fell at a London hotel bearing the name Hospitality Resorts of London on July 8, 1989. Panhandle, a semi-retired general practice physician, smashed his head on some marble flooring which was wet. The floor was next to the pool. A sign saying "slippery when wet" was set up next to the pool. Panhandle didn't see the sign. He crushed his head. He sustained severe and permanent injuries and was unable to practice medicine for two years.

Panhandle often stayed at the Hospitality Resorts. The resorts were known for cleanliness and hospitality. The staff was friendly and always helpful. The advertising for the resorts claimed that it was the "cleanest in the world. We stay on top of our hotels." Most advertisements stated that the hotels were independently owned and operated. Some ads, such as the one that appeared in the Doctor's Weekly, which Panhandle read, did not state that independent owners owned the London hotel. That ad boasted about the resort. "We care about you. We take care of you. We take care of your home - our resort."

Hospitality Resorts was a trade name. The company who licensed the name Hospitality Resorts to other hotels was called Hospitality Resorts International, Inc. (HRII), your client. Hospitality Resorts licensed the trade name of Hospitality Resorts to Fred and Ethel Carrigan of London, England for use in a hotel there. The Carrigan's called the hotel Hospitality Resorts of London. As part of the license agreement, Hospitality Resorts provided training to the staff. The Carrigans hired and fired the staff. HRII had no authority to hire and fire staff.

Panhandle did not know anything about the training or the connection between the London hotel and HRII. HRII provided operations manuals and suggested procedures and menus. Personnel from HRII regularly traveled to London to advise the hotel employees about their jobs. HRII had no ownership interest in the London hotel. HRII was not authorized to act on behalf of the hotel nor was the hotel authorized to act on behalf of HRII.

The license agreement between HRII and Hospitality Resort of London only provided for HRII to provide its name Hospitality Resort to the London hotel as well as some manuals and technical assistance. It did not authorize the London hotel to act as its agent and HRII was not an agent of the London hotel. HRII did include the Hospitality Resort of London in its list of Hospitality Resorts. That list appeared in many ads as well as in a brochure.

Plaintiff filed suit against the Hospitality Resort in London and Hospitality Resorts, and Hospitality Resorts International, Inc. alleging that HRII is in an agency relationship or apparent or ostensible agency relationship with the London Hospitality Resort. Thus, plaintiff claims that HRII and the London hotel are both responsible for his injuries. This suit was filed in the United States District Court for your area. All of the rules of that court and the Federal Rules of Civil Procedure apply.

Does our client have a good defense to the plaintiff's claim that it was in an agency relationship with the London hotel?

3.   Consider the following:

Nate Late, a business owner, has two partners in the operation of Loose Cannon Manufacturing in Gurnee Your state. He owns 33 1/3 parts of a $3 million company. Late is ill, but not dying. He is grooming a 26-year boy, Ivan T. All to run the business. He tells his family he likes the boy and that he wants to teach him the business. The business owner, Nate Late, dies. The most current will leaves the estate of Late to his wife, Shirley Late, and his only son, Lou Sier. All tells Mrs. Late that Late intended to give All Late's 1/3 interest in the company and that Late told All this on the day of his death in front of a banker. The conversation took place during a meeting and the agreement was never put into writing. Before this meeting, on the day of Late's death other employees of Loose Cannon heard Late say that he intended for All "to get" the business. Family members knew that Late intended for All to run the business and for All to get something if the business was sold. None of the family believed that Late intended to give the business to this newcomer. Late's shares of stock were never given to All. The shares were in the safe deposit box shared by Late and his wife of 24 years.

Rob R. Baron also claims that Late promised to give him the shares in the future. Baron admits that Late did not physically give him the shares before he died, but Baron insists that Late said "I shall give you my shares in two years."

Mrs. Late said that Mr. Late planned to give her the shares. He told her this when he opened the joint safety deposit box and gave her the key.

You work for a firm which has been retained by Mrs. Late. She would like to know if All can prove that Mr. Late gave All Mr. Late's interest in the company.

Draft an issue statement for the Late case.

Conclusion Drafting Exercises

4.   Assume that the statute in your state provides that Wakefield, the spouse, can renounce the will within six months of its admission to probate and that she would be entitled by statute to 1/3 of the estate and Grayson would be entitled to the remainder of the estate. Prepare a conclusion for the Wakefield problem.

5.   Assume that the highest court in your state has held that a hotel owner can be liable in a case similar to the one outlined in exercise 4. The liability is based upon the theory of apparent agency. Also assume that a decision of the federal appellate court in your area follows the your high court decision. Draft a conclusion for the problem outlined in Issue Drafting Exercise 2.

6.   Assume that the following statements are the law of the land concerning a gift. Draft a conclusion for the problem outline in Exercise 5.

A gift is a voluntary transfer of property from one person to another without any compensation or consideration. To be a valid gift, it must actually be made or executed. A gratuitous promise to make a gift in the future is not binding.

A living gift - a gift inter vivos.

Three elements are required for such a gift - donative intent, acceptance of the gifts and delivery.

These cases explain the elements of a living gift. They are binding authorities for this problem

---

Clark v. Davis: Clark told Davis, a friend, that after he got his life together, he would give Davis his coin collection. Until that time, Clark planned to use the collection and show it and maybe sell some of it. Court said that a donor must have a present mental capacity and intent to give away his property. Court held that there was no present intention to make a gift of the collection to Davis. Therefore, a gift was not made.

Wally v. Allan: Wally gave Allan a guitar for use in his rock band. The court found that Allan accepted the gift. When a gift, such as the guitar, is beneficial to the donee, acceptance is presumed.

Lois v. Kate: Lois told Kate that she planned to give her a CD. Kate asked when she would give it to her. Lois said that she would leave the CD at the front desk of her record company. Lois left the CD at the desk and did not mention that Kate needed to leave any money to pay for the CD. Therefore, the court said that delivery of a gift occurred when Lois left the CD at the front desk. Although delivery generally occurs when a party hands the gift over to the other party. The above situation also amounts to delivery.

Draft a conclusion for the problem outlined in Issue Drafting Exercise #3.

Applications

1.   Identify the Problems with these facts statements

a.   Ned and Wally Maine owned Whole In One Enterprises. Two former employees brought suit against Whole In One for sex discrimination. The Maines are subject to the jurisdiction of the statute if they are an employer. An employer, as defined by the statute, is one who is engaged in a business with fifteen or more employees working daily during twenty or more consecutive calendar weeks in the year which the discrimination occurred or the year preceding the discrimination. The plaintiffs, Cammy Ashton and Eve Kurth, also must be individuals employed by an employer, as defined by the statute.

b.   Whole In One operates a miniature golf course and restaurant between April and mid October each year. Whole In One had ten full-time employees and fourteen part-time employees in 1997 and 1998.

c.   Cammy Ashton was an independent contractor. She provided marketing services between October 1995 and August 1997. She was paid bi-weekly and received bonuses. Whole In One supplied her office supplies. She was fired in August 1997.

2.   Read the following statement. Make a list of the legally significant facts. Then prepare a facts statement for a memo which would explain the possible interests of all of the parties.

Make a note about the organization. What type of organization did you use and why?

Nate Late, a business owner, has two partners in the operation of Loose Cannon Manufacturing in Gurnee Your state. He owns 33 1/3 parts of a $3 million company. Late is ill, but not dying. He is grooming a 26-year boy, Ivan T. All to run the business. He tells his family he likes the boy and that he wants to teach him the business. The business owner, Nate Late, dies. The most current will leaves the estate of Late to his wife, Shirley Late, and his only son, Lou Sier. All tells Mrs. Late that Late intended to give All Late's 1/3 interest in the company and that Late told All this on the day of his death in front of a banker. The conversation took place during a meeting and the agreement was never put into writing. Before this meeting, on the day of Late's death other employees of Loose Cannon heard Late say that he intended for All "to get" the business. Family members knew that Late intended for All to run the business and for All to get something if the business was sold. None of the family believed that Late intended to give the business to this newcomer. Late's shares of stock were never given to All. The shares were in the safe deposit box shared by Late and his wife of 24 years.

Rob R. Baron also claims that Late promised to give him the shares in the future. Baron admits that Late did not physically give him the shares before he died, but Baron insists that Late said "I shall give you my shares in two years." Mrs. Late said that Mr. Late planned to give her the shares. He told her this when he opened the joint safety deposit box and gave her the key.

Mrs. Late retained your firm. She would like to know if All can prove that Mr. Late gave All Mr. Late's interest in the company.

Facts Drafting Exercises

3. Make a list of the legally significant facts.

You are a paralegal with the firm of Probing and Will. You must research whether Sarah Wakefield can renounce Adam Antwernts' will and collect a portion of the estate.

Your firm's client is Sarah Wakefield. She was married to Adam Antwernt. Antwernt died on June 6, 1998 in your state following a long illness. Wakefield was Antwernt's second wife. She had been married to him for more than 20 years and lived in their home in the Highlands of your state. Antwernt purchased the home with his first wife, Carry MacOver. MacOver died in 1965. When Antwernt married Wakefield he never changed the deed for the home to include Wakefield. Wakefield kept her maiden name. Antwernt adopted a son with MacOver in 1964. The son, who is now 34 years old, is Grayson Antwernt.

Antwernt drafted his will in May of 1992. He and his wife were getting along fine. However, he excluded her from his will. He did not leave her any property. Instead, he left all of his property to Grayson. Antwernt's will was admitted to probate on July 8, 1998.

Wakefield wants to whether Antwernt's will is valid and whether he can divest her of their marital property or whether she can renounce the will and collect a portion of the estate.

Grayson is out of town and his attorney told Wakefield that she will get her share of the estate once Grayson returns. He is scheduled to return on July 5, 1999.

Prepare a list of the legally significant facts. Then draft a facts statement for the above problem.

4.   Prepare a list of legally significant facts for the following scenario. Next, draft a facts statement.

Your client, Hospitality Resorts International, Inc., is defending an action against James Panhandle, a 70-year-old doctor from Akron, Ohio, who slipped and fell at a London hotel bearing the name Hospitality Resorts of London on July 8, 1998. Panhandle, a semi-retired general practice physician, smashed his head on some marble flooring which was wet. The floor was next to the pool. A sign saying "slippery when wet" was set up next to the pool. Panhandle didn't see the sign. He crushed his head. He sustained severe and permanent injuries and was unable to practice medicine for two years.

Panhandle often stayed at the Hospitality Resorts. The resorts were known for cleanliness and hospitality. The staff was friendly and always helpful. The advertising for the resorts claimed that it was the "cleanest in the world. We stay on top of our hotels." Most advertisements stated that the hotels were independently owned and operated. Some ads, such as the one that appeared in the Doctor's Weekly, which Panhandle read, did not state that independent owners owned the London hotel. That ad boasted about the resort. "We care about you. We take care of you. We take care of your home - our resort."

Hospitality Resorts actually was a trade name. The company who licensed the name Hospitality Resorts to other hotels was called Hospitality Resorts International, Inc. (HRII), our client. Hospitality Resorts licensed the trade name of Hospitality Resorts to Fred and Ethel Carrigan of London, England for use in a hotel there. The Carrigan's called the hotel Hospitality Resorts of London. As part of the license agreement, Hospitality Resorts provided training to the staff. The Carrigans hired and fired the staff. HRII had no authority to hire and fire staff.

Panhandle did not know anything about the training or the connection between the London hotel and HRII.

HRII provided operations manuals and suggested procedures and menus. Personnel from HRII regularly traveled to London to advise the hotel employees about their jobs. HRII had no ownership interest in the London hotel. HRII was not authorized to act on behalf of the hotel nor was the hotel authorized to act on behalf of HRII.

The license agreement between HRII and Hospitality Resort of London only provided for HRII to provide its name Hospitality Resort to the London hotel as well as some manuals and technical assistance. It did not authorize the London hotel to act as its agent and HRII was not an agent of the London hotel. HRII did include the Hospitality Resort of London in its list of Hospitality Resorts. That list appeared in many ads as well as in a brochure.

Plaintiff filed suit against the Hospitality Resort in London and Hospitality Resorts, and Hospitality Resorts International, Inc. alleging that HRII is in an agency relationship or apparent or ostensible agency relationship with the London Hospitality Resort. Thus, plaintiff claims that HRII and the London hotel are both responsible for his injuries. This suit was filed in the United States District Court for the Northern District of Your state. All of the rules of that court and the Federal Rules of Civil Procedure apply.

Does our client have a good defense to the plaintiff's claim that it was in an agency relationship with the London hotel? Can a claim of an apparent agency relationship be the basis of a personal injury action?

Chapter 22
Synthesizing Cases and Authorities

Application of Case Synthesis Concepts

1.   The fact pattern for the following questions is:

Ms. Jones was waiting to get off the commuter train in the train's vestibule. The commuter train pulled into the station and Ms. Jones descended the stairs to disembark from the train. The conductors exit the train first to watch the passengers exit the train and then signal to close the doors and for the train to start rolling. Ms. Jones was carrying her briefcase that had a long strap. As Ms. Jones exited the train the briefcase strap was behind her. The train doors shut with Ms. Jones on the platform but with the briefcase strap still inside the door. The train dragged Ms. Jones about 10 feet and she suffered a broken shoulder. The issue you have to consider is whether the conductor's negligence by signaling for the train to start was the proximate cause of Ms. Jones broken shoulder. The issue that you should focus your case synthesis on is whether the conductor's failure to see that Ms. Jones briefcase strap was inside the door as he signaled for the train to start moving is the proximate cause of her injury, her broken shoulder.

Read the two cases and answer the questions which follow.

Smith v. Atlantic City Railroad, 12 Nowhere 2d 5 (1994).
Mr. John Smith was injured on the Atlantic City Railroad when the train lurched with great violence as it rounded a curve on the track. The train was overcrowded. Smith was injured without fault on his part. The motorman drove the overcrowded car too fast around the curve, as to cause it to give a severe lurch. Where a passenger train is overcrowded and the employees operating the train know of such condition, it is their duty to exercise additional care commensurate with the dangers. The motorman knew of the overcrowded conditions and failed to exercise additional care when rounding the curve. Mr. Smith was injured when the train lurched as it rounded the curve because he fell on to another passenger. The motorman's failure to exercise the requisite care was the proximate cause of Mr. Smith's injuries.

Blue v. Boardwalk Railroad, 15 Nowhere 2d 9 (1980).
Mr. Robert Blue was blinded by a sudden gust of steam and fell underneath the train he was in the process of boarding at the station; Mr. Blue's arm was severed by the train as it started to leave the

station. Regular inspection of couplings is a required duty of conductors. Failure to inspect the couplings for leaks is a negligent act on the part of the defendant. Railroad's allowing steam to escape was the proximate cause of Mr. Blue's injury, since a man of ordinary prudence could have foreseen that escaping steam from would result from leaks in the uninspected couplings. The consequence of the escaping steam, due to the railroad's failure to inspect the couplings, resulted in a foreseeable injury to a passenger or person waiting on the platform.

a.   Brief the cases to extract the holdings.

b.   What are the similarities and differences between the <u>Blue</u> case and the <u>Smith</u> case?

c.   How do the facts differ?

d.   How do the holdings differ?

e.   What do the cases have in common?

f.   Formulate a statement of law that incorporates the holdings from the <u>Smith</u> case and the <u>Blue</u> case.

Application Exercises

1.   Please label the components of the discussion, which follows, to indicate Issue, Rule, Application and Conclusion and where each component begins.

The discussion is based on these facts:

Drake Industries has been leasing warehouse space at 2700 North Bosworth Avenue in Chicago, Illinois, from the owner of the building, Michael Martin. Drake began leasing space from Martin beginning January 1, 1969 at $700.00 per month until the lease expired on December 31, 1980.

Martin offered a new lease to Drake on November 25, 1980, to be signed and returned by December 31, 1980. The new lease began January 1, 1981 and expired on December 31, 1994, and the rent increased to $850.00 per month, payable on the first of each month. Drake never signed and never returned the new lease, but did pay the increased rent amount during the term of the unsigned lease ending December 31, 1994. Since then, Drake has continued paying $850.00 on the first day of each month. On August 15, 1995, Martin requested that Drake surrender the premises. Drake came to our firm to find out what type of tenancy he has and whether Martin gave Drake the proper notice to quit the premises.

Is Drake Industries is a holdover tenant? A holdover tenancy is created when a landlord elects to treat a tenant, after the expiration of his lease, as a tenant for another term upon the same provisions contained in the original lease. Bismarck Hotel Co. v. Sutherland, 92 Ill. App. 3d 167, 415 N.E.2d 517 (1980). In Bismarck, defendant Sutherland's written lease expired. Bismarck presented her with a new lease which included a rent increase. She began to pay the increase but did not sign the new lease. Sutherland could not be a holdover since the terms of the old lease were not extended to the terms of the new, unsigned lease. Drake Industries was offered anew lease in 1980, which included a rent increase. Since the terms were different from the original lease, Drake could not be considered a holdover tenant.

It is the intention of the landlord, not the tenant, that determines whether the tenant is to be treated as a holdover. Sheraton-Chicago Corp. v. Lewis, 8 Ill. App. 3d 309, 290 N.E.2d 685 (1972). When a landlord creats a new lease and presents it to the tenant, it is clear that it was his intention that a new tenancy was created. Holt v. Chicago Hair Goods Co., 328 Ill. App. 671, 66 N.E.2d 727 (1946). Martin presented Drake with a new lease to sign in November, 1980 with new terms beginning January 1, 1981. It was never his intention to hold over the same lease from 1969. Therefore, Drake was not a holdover tenant and has never been one. 735 ILCS 5/9-202 (West 1993) could not apply to Drake and Martin could not demand double rental fees from Drake when it remained in possession of 2700 W. Bosworth after the written lease expired on December 31, 1980.

Whether Drake Industries is a year-to-year tenant? When the payment of rent is annual, there arises a tenancy from year-to-year, even if the agreement provides for a payment of one-twelfth of the annual rental each month. Seaver Amusement Co. v. Saxe et al., 210 Ill. App. 289 (1918). The terms of the 1969 written lease would have to have said "$8,400.00 a year rent, payable in monthly installments of $700.00" for it to have been considered a year-to-year lease. Since the terms of the 1969 lease only provided for monthly payments and not a yearly rental rate, Drake was not a year-to -year tenant. 735 ILCS 5/9-205 (1993) does not apply at all to Drake, and Martin would not be required to tender 60 days' written notice to terminate the tenancy.

Whether Drake Industries is a month-to-month tenant? A month-to-month tenancy is created when a tenant remains in possession of the premises after a lease expires under different terms of tenancy. Bismarck at 167, 415 N.E.2d at 517. By paying Bismarck's increased rental amount, different terms of the tenancy were established, so Sutherland's tenancy was considered month-to-month by the court. Drake remained at 2700 N. Bosworth after its lease expired in 1980, but began paying the increased rent to Martin under the new terms of the unsigned lease. This established different terms of tenancy, so Drake has been a month-to-month tenant since 1980.

What type of tenancy is created under an oral lease? When a tenant goes into possession of real estate under a verbal leasing agreement for a term over one year at monthly rental, the agreement is voidable under the Statute of Frauds. The most that the tenant in possession can claim is that the leasing is from month-to-month and that the landlord can terminate the tenancy by providing 30 days' notice in writing to the tenant. Creighton v. Sanders, 89 Ill. 543 (1878). Charles Creighton had a verbal agreement to lease a house from Patrick Sanders for a five-year term. When Creighton ceased paying rent, Sanders gave him a written notice to quit the premises. Creighton maintained that he had a five-year lease, but the most the court allowed was that he was a month-to-month tenant, based on the parol lease. When Drake never signed and never returned the new lease in 1980, he entered into a parol lease agreement with Martin. Martin cannot hold Drake to any terms of that lease because the tenancy was for a duration of twelve years, well over the one year limit under the Statute of Frauds. The most Martin can claim is that Drake is a month-to-month tenant.

What type of notice is necessary to vacate the premises? Under 735 ILCS 5/9-207 (1993) notice to terminate a month-to-month tenancy must be made with a 30 days' notice, in writing, before any action for forcible entry and detainer can be maintained. Drake said that on August 15,

1995, Martin "requested" that Drake surrender the premises. An oral request may not be sufficient and Drake may maintain that proper notice has not been made and it need not surrender the premises by September 15, 1995. A forcible entry and detainer action could not be entered and maintained and Drake need not surrender the premises until proper notice has been given.

Drafting Exercises

2.   Write an IRAC paragraph based on the following facts, issue and cases.

The fact pattern is:

Ms. Jones was waiting to get off the commuter train in the train's vestibule. The commuter train pulled into the station and Ms. Jones descended the stairs to disembark from the train. The conductors exit the train first to watch the passengers exit the train and then signal to close the doors and for the train to start rolling. Ms. Jones was carrying her briefcase that had a long strap. As Ms. Jones exited the train the briefcase strap was behind her. The train doors shut with Ms. Jones on the platform but with the briefcase strap still inside the door. The train dragged Ms. Jones about 10 feet and she suffered a broken shoulder. The issue you have to consider is whether the conductor's negligence by signaling for the train to start was the proximate cause of Ms. Jones broken shoulder.

The issue that you should focus your case synthesis on is whether the conductor's failure to see that Ms. Jones briefcase strap was inside the door as he signaled for the train to start moving is the proximate cause of her injury, her broken shoulder.

Read the two cases:

Smith v. Atlantic City Railroad, 12 Nowhere 2d 5 (1994).
      Mr. John Smith was injured on the Atlantic City Railroad when the train lurched with great violence as it rounded a curve on the track. The train was overcrowded. Smith was injured without fault on his part. The motorman drove the overcrowded car too fast around the curve, as to cause it to give a severe lurch. Where a passenger train is overcrowded and the employees operating the train know of such condition, it is their duty to exercise additional care commensurate with the dangers. The motorman knew of the overcrowded conditions and failed to exercise additional care when rounding the curve. Mr. Smith was injured when the train lurched as it rounded the curve because he fell on to another passenger. The motorman's failure to exercise the requisite care was the proximate cause of Mr. Smith's injuries.

Blue v. Boardwalk Railroad, 15 Nowhere 2d 9 (1980).
      Mr. Robert Blue was blinded by a sudden gust of steam and fell underneath the train he was in the process of boarding at the station; Mr. Blue's arm was severed by the train as it started to

leave the station. Regular inspection of couplings is a required duty of conductors. Failure to inspect the couplings for leaks is a negligent act on the part of the defendant. Railroad's allowing steam to escape was the proximate cause of Mr. Blue's injury, since a man of ordinary prudence could have foreseen that escaping steam from would result from leaks in the uninspected couplings. The consequence of the escaping steam, due to the railroad's failure to inspect the couplings, resulted in a foreseeable injury to a passenger or person waiting on the platform.

3.   Write an IRAC paragraph based on the following facts, issue and statutes.

The fact pattern is:

Ms. Jones was waiting to get off the commuter train in the train's vestibule. The commuter train pulled into the station and Ms. Jones descended the stairs to disembark from the train. The conductors exit the train first to watch the passengers exit the train and then signal to close the doors and for the train to start rolling. Ms. Jones was carrying her briefcase which had a long strap. As Ms. Jones exited the train the briefcase strap was behind her. The train doors shut with Ms. Jones on the platform but with the briefcase strap still inside the door. The train dragged Ms. Jones about 10 feet and she suffered a broken shoulder. The issue you have to consider is whether the conductor's negligence by signaling for the train to start was the proximate cause of Ms. Jones broken shoulder.

The issue that you should focus your case synthesis on is whether the conductor's failure to see that Ms. Jones briefcase strap was inside the door as he signaled for the train to start moving is the proximate cause of her injury, her broken shoulder.

The statutes are:

Chapter 131 Nowhere Revised Code §12 (1991)
An operator of a common carrier must perform regular inspections of all components of the common carrier. Failure to do so constitutes negligence. The failure to perform inspections and the resulting negligence will be considered the proximate cause of all injuries occuring aboard a common carrier.

Chapter 131 Nowhere Revised Code §14 (1991)
It is the duty of an operator of a common carrier to exercise additional care when dangers are foreseeable.

Chapter 24
Outlining and Organizing a Memorandum

Research

1.   After you have reviewed the facts presented and the information available to you, map out your research strategy. What specific sources will you use? Indicate what you hope to learn from each source and what type of authority you will find in each source.

2.   Using the facts specified below, research the question of intentional infliction of emotional distress in your jurisdiction. Find answers only the questions presented in the memo below.

Outlining

3.   Next outline the discussion section. Provide a detailed outline and list of authorities. Incorporate your authorities into your outline. .

Drafting

4.   Write the discussion section only for the following memo.

MEMORANDUM

TO: Karen Abbey

FROM: Gail Mark

DATE: January 28, 1999

RE: <u>Kahn v. Randall</u>, Civ 95 No. 988, File No. 8988977

Question Presented:

    Does Janice Kahn have a valid claim for intentional infliction of emotional distress against Ronnie Randall after Kahn saw Randall turn his car to strike Kahn's 11-year-old child in front of her causing her to suffer from anxiety, headaches and vomiting?

Conclusion:

    Janice Kahn probably has a valid claim for intentional infliction of emotional distress against Ronnie Randall. Kahn saw Randall turn his car to strike her 11-year-old child. Seeing this accident caused Kahn to suffer from anxiety, headaches and vomiting daily. This act could be considered extreme and outrageous conduct if it was done with intent. Several witness can testify that Randall said that he intended to harm Kahn and Kahn states that Randall turned the car to strike her son. Two factors, however, might show that Randall lacked intent: the statement that he made to the police that he did not intend to hit the child and the fact that his blood alcohol level was .11 possibly preventing him from formulating the needed intent.

Facts:

    While driving a car Ronnie Randall struck Janice Kahn's son at 5 p.m. on August 29, 1998. It was bright and clear. No skid marks appeared on the dry street following the accident.

    Janice Kahn was working in her garden about five feet from the accident scene at the time of the accident. Her son was playing a game in the street before Randall's car struck him. Kahn did not see the car strike her 11-year-old son. When she first looked up from her garden, she thought her son was dead. He was covered with blood and had several broken bones. However, Kahn's son was conscious after the accident.

Immediately after the accident, Randall, who had a blood alcohol level of .11, was cited for drunk driving and driving with a suspended driver's license. Police charged him with drunk driving and suspended his license two weeks earlier after the car he was driving struck another child at the same spot. Randall has a drinking history.

Following the accident, several witnesses said Randall was upset and wobbled as he walked. One witness said that Randall intentionally turned the steering wheel to his Kahn's son. Kahn stated that Randall often swerved down her street to get her attention.

Rhonda Albert, Kahn's neighbor, said she heard Randall say he would get even with Kahn after Kahn broke off a 10-year relationship with him.

During Kahn and Randall's 10-year relationship, Randall was close to Kahn's son. He took him to ballgames, including one in April, and attended the son's baseball games. Randall knew that Kahn's son was the most important person in her life.

Since the accident, Kahn vomits up daily and has nightmares about the accident. Dr. Susan Faigen, Kahn's internist states that the vomiting and nightmares are the result of the accident.

Research Memo

5.   Read the statement below. Research the issues asked and then prepare a 6 page typed memo. Be sure that it is double-spaced. The jurisdiction for this problem is your state. Be sure to consult the exercise in Chapter 14 for assistance in how to complete the research portion of the project.

You are a paralegal with the Law Office of Warren T. Sales. You have been asked to research the following questions and provide answers. These are the facts that Mr. Sales presented to you.

Your client is Sue A. Seller. She lives at 3225 Wilmette Avenue, Glenview, Your state. The defendants are Lee R. Merchant, owner of Mowers R Us, in Glenview, Your state, and Manny U. Facture, the owner of a manufacturing concern which is not incorporated called Mowers, of Rosemont, Your state. Ms. Seller went to the defendant's store, Mowers R Us, to purchase a lawnmower for her new home. She was a first-time homeowner. She was unfamiliar with lawnmowers. She had never operated a lawnmower because her brothers always had mowed the lawn when she was a child.

When she went to Mowers R Us, she asked to speak with the owner. "I want to speak only to the owner," she told Mr. Merchant. "I don't know anything about these mowers and I need to talk with an expert." Mr. Merchant said, "I'm the owner and you couldn't find a better expert anywhere in the Chicagoland area. I have been in the business of selling mowers for more than 40 years. I only sell mowers and the equipment to clean and repair them. Are you familiar with the type of lawnmower you would like?," Mr. Merchant added.

"No, I don't know anything about lawnmowers. I just know that I have to have a lawnmower that will mulch my grass clippings because I cannot bag the clippings. The village of Glenview does not permit me to bag the clippings. So the clippings must remain on my lawn," Ms. Seller told Mr. Merchant.

"You're absolutely correct. You must have a mulching mower," Mr. Merchant said. "That type of mower will grind the grass clippings and you will not notice them on your grass."

"I have the perfect mower for you," Mr. Merchant continued. "It is a used model that will fit into your price range. It is only $200. It is a good brand a Roro. It will mulch the grass as well as any of the new mowers. This one is true blue. You can purchase a separate mulching blade which will easily attach to it for an additional $50," he added.

"Do you think that I need the mulching blade," Ms. Seller asked, "I've never used a lawnmower so I don't know what to expect and you appear to be the expert."

"I think that you could do without the mulching blade unless you want the grass ground up very fine," Mr. Merchant said.

"I think that I would like it ground up fine. I'll defer to your judgment. If you think a mulching blade is necessary, then I'll buy that with the mower. Do you think that this is the best mower for mulching?," asked Ms. Seller.

"Absolutely, I told you it is a true value. It will mulch with the best of them," Mr. Merchant said.

"If you think it can do the job, I'll trust your judgment," said Ms. Seller. "I'll take the mower and the mulching blade. Can you install the mulching blade. I don't know anything about the installation."

"Sure, we can install any blade for another $30.00," Mr. Merchant said.

"OK. Do you clean up the machine, too?," Ms. Seller asked.

"We can do it for an additional $40 or you can do it yourself with the special industrial strength, non-toxic, non-irritant mower cleaner," Mr. Merchant told Ms. Seller.

"Well I have sensitive skin, do you really think that the mower cleaner is safe for me to use? I have never used any type of industrial strength cleaner, Ms. Seller said.

"Absolutely, I've used the cleaner many times and it is very safe and won't hurt your sensitive skin at all."

Ms. Seller purchased the mower, the blade and the cleaner. She used the mower after Mr. Merchant installed the new mulching blade. It barely cut the grass and certainly didn't mulch the clippings into fine pieces as Mr. Merchant had claimed.

She brought the mower back to Mr. Merchant. He said that he had made no warranties about the mower. He showed her the language on the receipt which said that he did not expressly warrant anything.

Ms. Seller brought the mower to a Roro dealer. The owners of the Roro dealership, Abe Saul and Lou T. Wright, said that the mower Ms. Seller had purchased from Mowers R Us was not a mulching mower. It was a mower built before mulching was popular. Therefore, it would not perform the mulching task. It was designed merely to cut the grass. "Any merchant who has been in business for one year or more should have known that mowers built before 1970 were not designed for mulching," Mr. Wright said. He showed Ms. Seller where the manufacturing date appeared on the mower. "Manufactured in August 1969," it said on the plate with the serial number. "Also, mulching blades cannot be placed on these old mowers. Any mower dealer should know that too," Mr. Wright added. "However, this mower isn't defective. It can cut the grass without mulching it."

The mower wasn't Ms. Seller's only problem. She also had used the cleaner with gloves. She broke out in rash all over her hands. The dermatologist stated that the cleaner was caustic and permeated the gloves, causing the rash on Ms. Seller's hands.

Ms. Seller is bringing an action against Mr. Merchant and Mr. Facture in the trial court in your state. Your research is limited to actions Ms. Seller has against Mr. Merchant for breach of an implied warranty of fitness for a particular purpose.

6.   You are a paralegal with the firm of Probing and Will. You must research whether Sarah Wakefield can renounce Adam Antwernts' will and collect a portion of the estate.

Your firm's client is Sarah Wakefield. She was married to Adam Antwernt. Antwernt died on June 6, 1998 in your state following a long illness. Wakefield was Antwernt's second wife. She had been married to him for more than 20 years and lived in their home in the Highlands of your state. Antwernt purchased the home with his first wife, Carry MacOver. MacOver died in 1965. When Antwernt married Wakefield he never changed the deed for the home to include Wakefield. Wakefield kept her maiden name. Antwernt adopted a son with MacOver in 1964. The son, who is now 30 years old is Grayson Antwernt.

Antwernt drafted his will in May of 1992. He and his wife were getting along fine. However, he excluded her from his will. He did not leave her any property. Instead, he left all of his property to Grayson. Antwernt's will was admitted to probate on July 8, 1998.

Wakefield wants to whether Antwernt's will is valid and whether he can divest her of their marital property or whether she can renounce the will and collect a portion of the estate.

Grayson is out of town and his attorney told Wakefield that she will get her share of the estate once Grayson returns. He is scheduled to return on July 5, 1999.

What rights does Mrs. Wakefield have to the estate? How must she exercise those rights in your state? Draft a research memo to address these point.

For the following exercises, assume that you are a paralegal with the law firm of Williams, Kurth and Taylor, 30 N. Wacker Drive, Chicago, Illinois, 60606. The phone number is 312-792-3161.

1.   Prepare a letter to attorney Gene Williams of the Law Office of Gene Williams, 20 E. Washington Street, Chicago, Illinois, 60611. You want to tell Mr. Herring that you are sending him a copy of a real estate contract between your clients, Laura and James Hirsh, and his clients, Michelle and Jordan Bream for the purchase of 2525 Canterbury Lane, Glenview, Illinois 60025. You also are including a $41,000 certified check for the escrow for the property. This represents 10 percent of the purchase price. The closing is tentatively set for April 1 of this year. The letter is being hand-delivered by a messenger from your law firm. The letter is being typed by your secretary Carly Alice Connelly. A blind copy is being sent to the partner on the case, Wally Taylor.

2.   You are responsible for mailing interrogatories to the plaintiff's lawyer, Karen Watkins at the Law Office of Karen Watkins 25 E. Randolph Street, Chicago, Illinois 60611. You complete the interrogatories on October 30 of this year at 11 p.m. What date should you put on the letter and what date will the letter be mailed. Draft this letter. Your secretary Carly Alice Connelly will be typing the letter and a carbon copy should be sent to the partner Alicia Coffield.

3.   You are sending a letter via facsimile and U.S. mail to Beth Baker, 30 S. Taylor Street, Milwaukee, Wisc. Baker works at Baker, Corvino and German. This letter is to confirm negotiations for the purchase of a business Hocking Enterprises in Brown Deer, Wisconsin. The negotiations are set for 10 a.m. at your offices on June 12 of this year. You expect that your clients, Kenny and Margaret Hocking will be at your office and that Ms. Baker will be bringing her clients. The partner on the case is Wally Taylor. His secretary Jan Marie Maggio is typing you letter and will make certain that Mr. Taylor receives a copy of the letter. Draft the letter.

4.   You are assigned to prepare a letter that explains the status of a pending insurance defense litigation matter. The matter is set for trial on November 15 of this year. Two depositions have been taken. The plaintiff's and the defendant's depositions. Interrogatories have been answered by both sides and a settlement conference is scheduled with the judge in the case. The judge is Theodore G. Halsey of Ohio Common Pleas Court in Columbus Ohio. You expect that a representative of the restaurant where the incident took place will attend the settlement conference and that an insurance company representative also will attend as required by the local court rules. Your firm will be calling several witnesses from the restaurant to testify at the trial and you and the partner on the case, Wally Taylor, will be preparing these witnesses to testify beginning in October. Send this letter to your client, Cosco Insurance Enterprise, 250 W. Wilson Street, Wilmette, Ill. 60091. The

person you deal with at the Insurance company is Thomas Kennedy, a claims manager. You are sending this letter via Express Mail. The letter is being typed to Taylor's secretary Jan Marie Maggio. She will send a blind copy of the letter to an associate on the case, Janis Harris. She also will send a carbon copy of the letter to Mr. Taylor.

5.   Draft a letter to Barry and Debbie Williams telling them that you are sending them a copy of their wills and a living trust. These are their signed copies for their files. Tell them to place these documents in a safe place and that you will keep copies at your office. Thank them for allowing your firm to handle this matter and tell them that you are looking forward to working with them on setting up a new business enterprise during the next year. Send a copy of the letter to Wally Taylor and to the associate Janis Harris. The letter is being typed by your secretary, Carly Alice Connelly. The date of the letter should be today's date. This letter is being sent by Federal Express.

Basic Concepts -- Citation Exercises

1.   For the following citation, <u>Sloan v. Walker</u>, 671 F. Supp. 325 (D.N.J. 1987), please provide the following:

      a.   The plaintiff's name:

      b.   The defendant's name:

      c.   The volume number:

      d.   The reporter:

      e.   The page number where the case can be found:

      f.   The court and what its abbreviation means:

      g.   The year of decision:

Application of Concepts – Citation Exercises

For the following citations, assume that these cases are being used in a brief for the U.S. District Court for the Northern District of Ohio. Correct the citation if possible. If not, please specific what is wrong. if an item is missing note it and where it belongs.

1.   How would you cite the following slip opinion? Michele Greear, et. al., plaintiffs, vs. C.E. Electronics, Inc., et. al., defendants, decided in the United States District Court for the Northern District of Ohio Western Division, docket number C 87-7749, decided by Judge Richard B. McQuade, Jr. on September 11, 1989.

2.   When responding to a motion for summary judgment, the plaintiff must submit proof of each and every element of his claims so that a reasonable jury would find in his favor. <u>Anderson v. Liberty Lobby, Inc.</u>, 477 U.S. 242, 105 S.Ct. 989, 10 L.E.2d 1111 (1986).

3.   When the relationship of the parties is so clear as to be undisputed, it can be decided as a matter of law that no apparent or actual relationship existed. <u>Mateyka</u> <u>v.</u> <u>Schroeder</u>, 504 N.E.2d 1289 (1987).

4.   In a diversity action, a court must apply the conflict of law principles of the forum state. <u>Dr.</u> <u>Franklin Perkins School v. Freeman</u>, 741 F2d 1503, 1515, n.19 (1984); Pittway Corp. v. Lockheed Aircraft Corp., 641 F.2d 524, 526 (7th Cir.) ; Klaxon Co. v. Stentor Electric Mfg. Co., 313 US 487, 496 (1941);

5.   Gizzi v. Texaco, 437 F.2d 308 (3rd).

6.   Zimmerman v. North American, 704 F.2d 347 (1983)

7.   E.E.O.C. v. Dowd, 736 F.2d 1177

8.   Musser v. Mountain View Broadcasting, 578 F. Supp. 229 (1984)

Citation Exercises

Please provide the correct citations for these problems.

1.   Plaintiffs have elected to resist the motion for summary judgment by trying to create issues, involving immaterial facts rather that the "material" facts emphasized by Rule 56, F.R.C.P.

2.   A complaint must be dismissed if a claim is lacking. Federal Rule of Civil Procedure 12 b.

3.   How would you cite rule 803 of the Federal Rules of Evidence?

4.   How would you cite rule 22 of the U.S. Supreme Court Rules?

5.   How would you cite Federal Rule of Appellate Procedure 10?

6.   United States v. Upjohn, 449 U.S. 383

7.   Indicate what, if anything, is missing from this citation: Consolidation Coal Co. v. Bueyrus-Erie Co., 89 Ill. App. 2d 103 (1982).